WHEREABOUTS UNKNOWN

20 MYSTERIOUS MISSING PERSON CASES

JENN BAXTER

ISBN: 9798853045880
Copyright 2023 by Jenn Baxter

Cases:

1. Cynthia Anderson
2. David Blockett
3. Robert John Bornos
4. Diana Braungardt
5. Lynn Burdick
6. Susan Wolff Cappel
7. Brenda Condon
8. Jennifer Fay
9. Darla Harper
10. Tomiene Jones
11. Bethany Markowski
12. Nita Mayo
13. Jennifer Pandos
14. Bianca Piper
15. Felipe Santos & Terrance Williams
16. Nefertiri Trader
17. Daffany Tullos
18. Darlene Webb
19. Brandi Wells
20. Alan & Terry Westerfield

Cynthia Anderson

Cynthia Anderson was in a hurry to get to work on the morning of August 4, 1981. The 20-year-old skipped breakfast, told her parents she would see them later, and rushed out the door of their Lambertville, Michigan home at 8:30 am. Cindy was employed as a secretary in a law office in Toledo, Ohio; her morning commute usually took her approximately 20 minutes, and that day was no different.

Cindy pulled into the shopping center where the Neller & Rabbit legal center was located at 8:50 am and parked her Chevy Citation close to the front door. She unlocked the door and let herself inside, making sure to lock the door behind her. The lawyers who worked in the office were all at court that morning, so Cindy had the office to herself.

It was an extremely hot and humid day, and Cindy turned the air conditioner on so the office would be nice and cool by the time her boss and other lawyers started to arrive. She turned the radio on low and then settled in at her desk. Through the large plate glass window, Cindy had a view of the parking lot and door to the office, but she didn't expect to see any clients until later that day when the lawyers had returned from court.

Mornings were usually a relatively calm time for Cindy; in between answering phone calls, she occupied herself by reading a paperback romance novel. It was a routine she had grown used to, but one which was going to come to an end soon. Cindy had recently let her boss

5

know that she was leaving secretarial work in order to start attending classes at the William Tyndale Bible College in Detroit.

Cindy was excited about starting classes, especially since she was going to be attending college with her boyfriend, Jeff Lehmke. Cindy had been raised as a devout Christian fundamentalist, and though she hadn't dated a lot, she was certain that Jeff was going to be the man she married.

Cindy's mother tried to call her at the office sometime around 10:00 am but had been unable to reach anyone. She wasn't overly concerned; she assumed that Cindy was on the other line with a client and would call her later.

Around noon, two of the law partners returned to the office following a morning court session. James Rabbit and Jay Feldstein were happy to see that the air conditioning was on, as the temperature outside was close to 90 degrees. There were phone messages on their desks and everything in the reception area was immaculate as usual, but there was no sign of Cindy. Although it was unlike her to leave the office without putting a note on the door letting clients know when she would be back, they assumed she might have been in a hurry to get to lunch and had simply forgotten.

When the two men discovered that Cindy's car was still sitting in the parking lot, they grew concerned. If she had gone anywhere for lunch, she most likely would have driven there. When they noticed that she hadn't placed the phones on hold like she usually did whenever she had to step out, they began to worry that something might have happened to her. James reached down and picked up the romance novel that Cindy had left open on her desk and glanced idly at the pages, then felt a chill when he realized what he was looking at. The book was left open at the only violent passage it contained, where the lead character was abducted at knifepoint and feared she was about to die.

While the discovery of a violent passage in a romance novel wouldn't have meant much to most, everyone in the office was aware of the fact that Cindy had spent the past year living in fear that someone was out to get her. It had started with a series of violent dreams; in most, Cindy would open her front door to a man she knew, only to have him force her from her home and then murder her. The dreams had terrified Cindy, but her mother had tried to assure her that they were only dreams and didn't mean anything. They seemed to worsen over time, though, and it got to the point where Cindy was afraid to sleep.

Cindy's fears of a stalker had kicked into high gear when someone spray-painted "I love you, Cindy" on a cement wall that was visible from the window where Cindy sat at work. It had been painted over at one point but appeared again within a week or two. The initials "CJ + GW" had also been painted in several different spots. Cindy, whose middle name was Jane, had no idea who GW was but feared that he might be stalking her.

Her fear intensified when she started getting phone calls at work that seemed to terrify her, though she didn't tell anyone what the person on the other end of the line said. The day before she vanished, a client of the law firm had witnessed this fear. Larry Mullins had come in to pay his legal bill and had been chatting with Cindy while he wrote out a check. The phone rang, and Cindy answered it in her normal cheerful voice, then quickly slammed the phone down. A few seconds later, it rang again. Cindy sounded a bit more tentative when she answered it, and again slammed the receiver down.

Noting that she appeared to be completely petrified, Larry asked Cindy if everything was okay, and she forced herself to smile and told him that she was fine. When he tried to press her for more information, she admitted that the calls had been happening a lot recently, but refused to say anything else.

Larry paid his bill and drove home, but was so concerned by how terrified the young secretary had looked that he called the police from his house. He told them that something had scared the hell out of Cindy, and asked if they could have a patrol car drive through the shopping center to make sure she was okay. Even years later, Larry told reporters that he could still remember the look of fear on Cindy's face and noted that it gave him the chills just to think about it. It's unclear if police were dispatched to the shopping center that day.

Cindy had been so fearful of being the only person in the office that her boss had installed a special buzzer at her desk. If she got into any kind of trouble, she could use the buzzer to quickly alert employees who worked in the business next to the law firm, and they would immediately respond. Having the buzzer seemed to give Cindy some peace of mind, but she was always careful to make sure that she kept the door to the office locked so no one would be able to enter unseen.

Aware of the fear Cindy had been living in, James Rabbit called her home to see if any of them had heard from Cindy that day. Once he confirmed that no one knew where the secretary was, he called the police and reported her missing.

To their credit, the Toledo Police Department treated the case seriously from the very beginning. Although Cindy was an adult, and free to come and go as she pleased, there was nothing in her background that suggested she was the kind of person who would voluntarily run away. They searched through the law offices but found nothing to indicate that there had been any kind of a struggle. They didn't find Cindy's purse or her keys, but they were the only items that appeared to be missing.

Although Cindy had been alone in the office that morning, detectives were able to find two people who saw her. A maintenance man for the shopping center recalled seeing her enter the building around 8:50 am, and a woman who had walked past the law office at 9:45 am had glanced inside to check the time on a clock in the law office and saw Cindy sitting at her desk at that time. By 10:00 am, clients reported that no one had been answering the phone in the office. Whatever happened to Cindy had happened around 10:00 am.

Detectives interviewed all the people who worked in the law office; while most were able to confirm the fact that Cindy had been growing increasingly fearful over the past several months, none of them were able to offer any insight into what might have happened to her.

Cindy's family, boyfriend, and friends were all questioned, and all reiterated that, despite her fears that someone was stalking her, Cindy had appeared to be looking forward to the future and was excited about starting Bible college. She was close with her family and had a large network of friends, and none of them believed that she would have voluntarily run away to start a new life somewhere.

Detectives were inclined to agree. The only thing Cindy had taken with her was her purse; her brand-new car, all her clothing and makeup, and all other personal belongings were left behind. She had taken $5.00 out of her bank account earlier that week, but it had been untouched since then. They searched through the family's Lambertville home but found nothing to indicate that Cindy had been planning to disappear. Cindy was known for being extremely straight-laced; she would call her parents if she was going to be a few minutes late getting home. Investigators believed that she had run into foul play, but they had no idea who might have wanted to hurt her.

Investigators looked into the graffiti that kept appearing near Cindy's office; they were extremely interested in learning who "G.W." was and if he had anything to do with Cindy's disappearance. Eventually, they were able to locate a man who admitted that he was the person who kept confessing his love for Cindy in spray paint, but he had never heard of Cindy Anderson. His girlfriend was named Cindy, and the messages were for her. It was just a coincidence that Cindy Anderson worked nearby; she had been fearful of the messages for no reason at all.

Detectives were aware of the frightening phone calls that Cindy had apparently been getting at work, but they were unable to develop any solid leads on where they were coming from. No one else in the office reported any calls after Cindy disappeared, and they were unable to trace the ones that had been made before she went missing.

A large-scale search was conducted of the area surrounding the shopping center where Cindy was last seen, but nothing was found. Toledo Police then expanded the search to include known dumping grounds throughout the city; Cindy's boyfriend and many other friends assisted police as they combed through parts of the city where Cindy never would have gone on her own. They were aware that if they found her in any of the areas where they were looking, she wasn't going to be alive.

The holiday season came and went, but there was little for the Anderson family to celebrate. Detectives admitted that they had exhausted all leads but were no closer to finding Cindy than they had been on the day she vanished. They continued to follow up on any tips that came in, but they were few and far between and never led to any real developments.

For years, there was no progress on the case. Even the prospect of a $10,000 reward failed to bring in any leads. Detectives were certain that Cindy had met with foul play, but they still had no evidence to prove their theory and no suspects in her presumed murder. This changed in 1995, when investigators announced that they believed Cindy had been killed by Richard Neller, an attorney who had been one of her bosses at the time she went missing. In June 1995, Richard was one of nine people arrested in connection with a cocaine ring that police believed had been operating in the Toledo area since 1978. Richard was close friends with the ringleader of the group, Jose Rodriguez, and acted as his advisor in connection with his drug business. Federal prosecutors theorized that Cindy had overheard a conversation between the two men regarding one of their drug deals and had been abducted and killed so that she wouldn't be able to tell anyone.

There was no physical evidence linking either of the two men to Cindy's disappearance and murder, and they vehemently denied having anything to do with it. A federal drug task force spent three days searching the area around a Perrysburg pond looking for Cindy's body but found nothing to indicate that she had ever been there. Their information, which had apparently come from a jail informant looking to reduce his sentence, appeared to be faulty. Although Richard Neller and Jose Rodriguez would remain persons of interest, neither of them has ever been charged in connection with Cindy's disappearance.

Cindy's disappearance remains unsolved, and there are several different theories that have been put forth to explain it. It's very possible that she was abducted and murdered, though the idea that Richard Neller had her murdered for allegedly overhearing something seems shaky at best. The summer of 1981 was a particularly violent one in Toledo, and in the months before Cindy disappeared, three of the four murders police were working on dealt with victims who worked in the same shopping center that Cindy did. Some believe Cindy may have witnessed a robbery or other crime – from her desk, she could see everything going on in the shopping center, but people could see her as well – and was killed because of it. There is simply no evidence to prove or disprove any one theory.

Although none of her friends and family wanted to think it was possible, there is always a chance that Cindy did voluntarily leave home. Perhaps she never had any dreams or phone calls, but made them up to deflect people from realizing that she was planning to run off. She was raised in a strict fundamentalist household, and though she never seemed to act out or rebel in any way, her father noted that she had started skipping breakfast to spend more time on her makeup during the summer of 1981. Perhaps she had a new boyfriend and ran off to start a new life with him. It's unlikely, but an attractive alternative to her being dead.

Police still believe that foul play was involved in Cindy's disappearance and that she was most likely killed shortly after she went missing, Although her mother died of cancer in 1983 and her father died in 2006, Cindy still has family and friends in the Toledo area who miss her and hope to one day learn what happened to her.

Cynthia Jane Anderson was just 20 years old when she went missing from Lambertville, Michigan in August 1981. She had brown eyes and brown hair, and at the time of her disappearance, she was 5 feet 4 inches tall and weighed 115 pounds. She was last seen wearing a white dress with pink stripes, cinnamon brown Legg's pantyhose, and beige open-toed sandals. She has a chicken pox scar on her forehead and a fishhook-shaped scar on the inside of her right knee. If you have any information about Cindy, please contact the Toledo Police Department at 419-245-3111.

David Blockett

Vanessa Blockett, a 19-year-old mother of two, was startled by a knock at the front door of her Newport News, Virginia home on the morning of December 11, 1980. Neither she nor her mother, Shirley Blockett, had been expecting company that day. Shirley answered the door and found a woman who introduced herself as Marie Kelly, a social worker. Marie said she was from the Social Services Bureau and worked out of Riverside Regional Hospital; she was looking for David Blockett.

David, Vanessa's youngest son, was only 15 days old. Marie explained to Vanessa and Shirley that she had been sent to pick up David for the annual Christmas party held at Riverside Regional Hospital for all the children that had been born there. She seemed slightly perplexed when she realized the two women had no idea what she was talking about, and showed them a list of names. Sure enough, David's name was on the list, as were the names of several other children who lived in the neighborhood. Vanessa told Marie she had an older son as well, 2-year-old Frederick. Although his name wasn't on the list, Marie said he was certainly welcome to come along. In addition to the Christmas party, the hospital was also having a photo contest. All the children in attendance would get their picture taken and it would be printed in the local newspaper.

David was too young to comprehend what was going on, but Frederick grew excited at the thought of going to a party. Smiling at his enthusiasm, Vanessa gave her permission for both boys to go to the party. She made sure they were both dressed warmly, then bundled them up in their winter coats. Marie told them that she still had to pick up a couple more children who were on the list, and she would bring everyone back as soon as the party was over. Vanessa hugged and kissed her sons, then handed David over to Marie. She told Frederick to have fun as he bounced out the door and excitedly followed Marie to her car.

Vanessa stood in the doorway and waved until the car was out of sight. She and Shirley then sat down to enjoy the unexpected peace and quiet. The women had been chatting for about an hour when Vanessa got a phone call from the Hampton Police Department. A woman had found Frederick wandering alone near the Todd Center shopping plaza in Hampton, about 10 miles away from Newport News. He had a note in his pocket that had his name and address written on it. There was no sign of David.

Vanessa felt paralyzed with fear, barely able to process what she heard. After making sure that the Hampton police were going to bring Frederick home, Vanessa hung up with them and called the Newport News police. She told them that she believed her 15-day-old son had been kidnapped, and they immediately sent an officer to the house to take a report.

It didn't take long for police to confirm that there was no social worker named Marie Kelly working for either Riverside Regional Hospital or the Social Services Bureau. Nor had there been any sort of Christmas party taking place at the hospital. Shirley and Vanessa had fallen prey to an imposter, and she now had Vanessa's baby.

The women described Marie as a black woman, 30 to 35 years old, standing about 5 feet 6 inches tall and weighing approximately 150 pounds. She had a medium brown complexion, smooth skin without any scars, and a medium build with wide hips. Her black hair was short and straight, and she had arched eyebrows and straight, even teeth. She had been wearing a photo identification badge with the name Marie Kelly on it.

Police immediately released a sketch of the woman and asked the public to be on the lookout for her. They also released a picture of David, noting that he had a small mole the size of a pinhead inside his right ear and a birthmark under his right arm.

Local and state police, along with the FBI, organized a massive search for the missing infant. While they were canvassing the neighborhood, they spoke to a young mother who told them a woman fitting Marie's description had stopped by her home early that morning trying to pick up her child for a Christmas party. This mother had sensed something was off and told the woman to go away. The woman had given birth around the same time as Vanessa Blockett; it seemed that Marie was specifically targeting infants. Detectives realized that, three days earlier, the local paper had published a list of recent births. It gave each new baby's name, date of birth, and address; it made the perfect shopping list for a kidnapper.

The FBI had an agent stationed inside the Blockett home in case they received a ransom call. Everyone jumped when the phone rang late that afternoon, and Vanessa had to compose herself before answering. The call was from a woman, and she wanted to know what kind of baby formula David had been using. Unfortunately, the woman hung up before agents were able to trace the call. They were certain that the call had come from the kidnapper, and though it was somewhat disconcerting, the fact that she was asking about David's nutritional needs was a positive sign. Investigators believed the woman had likely taken the child so she could raise him as her own, and that meant that David was still alive. They just had to find him.

The FBI offered a reward for information in the case, and detectives were flooded with tips. They worked around the clock, meticulously following up on every lead they received. Each one led only to a dead end. Days turned to weeks, and the number of tips started to diminish. Investigators continued to vigorously seek out leads and possible suspects, but despite their hard work, the case started to go cold.

On December 23, a tourist found David's diaper bag on the side of Colonial Parkway near Yorktown. Inside were some of David's clothes, booties, and a blanket, as well as a hair comb that might have belonged to the kidnapper. The items in the bag were clean, and there was nothing to indicate that David had been injured. It was a positive sign, but it didn't bring them any closer to finding David. It was the only tangible piece of evidence that has ever been found in the case.

It's still unknown what happened to David that day. It's possible that Marie raised him as her own son. It's likely he's still alive and has no idea that he was kidnapped as an infant. Some investigators initially believed that David had been taken for the purpose of being sold into human trafficking or on the black market, but if this were the case the kidnapper likely would have kept Frederick as well. The fact that she wrote down Frederick's name and address before leaving him near a shopping center shows that she wanted him to be found and returned to his mother. This small amount of compassion is not something that would be expected from someone involved in human trafficking.

Frederick has only vague memories of what happened to him that day. He does remember sitting in the backseat of the car with David next to him, and he remembers playing with a cassette tape he found inside the vehicle. He believes that the car was driven by a man, and Marie sat in the passenger seat. He continues to wonder what happened to his baby brother and is hopeful they will one day be reunited.

Vanessa never gave up on the hope that she would one day find David. Unfortunately, she died suddenly from a brain aneurysm in 1997; she was only 36 years old. Some believe the stress of losing David may have contributed to her early death.

Newport News detectives recently reopened David's case, and they were pleased to learn that his diaper bag had been perfectly preserved in the evidence room. DNA testing was not available at the time David went missing in 1980, but investigators did preserve hair samples from the comb found in the bag. They plan to submit these for DNA testing to see if it brings them any closer to identifying the kidnapper.

David Ezell Blockett was only 15 days old when he was abducted from his home in Newport News, Virginia in December 1980. He has brown eyes and black hair; he also had a tiny mole on his right ear when he was born. It's possible David was raised by someone who may not have known that he was stolen from his mother; he was likely renamed and has gone through life not knowing he was adopted. If you have any information about David, please contact the Newport News Police Department at 757-926-8706.

Robert John Bornos

Robert John Bornos had started a new job on April 19, 1993, and was in a great mood when he returned home that afternoon. The 25-year-old, who was called Link by his family and friends, was currently separated from his wife and had been spending most nights at his mother's house in Cordova, Maryland. He had been hired as a caretaker of a private property in Trappe, Maryland, and he seemed excited about it. He told his mother, Linda Blizzard, that he had enjoyed his first day of work, and thought he was really going to like his new job.

After eating dinner with his mother, he told her was going out with some of his friends that evening to celebrate his new job. He showered and put on blue jeans and a t-shirt with the name of one of his favorite bands, The Who, emblazoned on the front of it. He told his mother that he and his friends were going to play some pool at the Choptank Inn on Route 50 in Easton, Maryland. It was one of their regular hangouts; they liked being able to shoot some pool while enjoying drinks from the bar.

Linda asked her son if he planned to come back home that night, or if he was going to stay at his sister's house, and Link told her he would call her later that evening to let her know. Although he spent a lot of time at his mother's home, he would also occasionally stay with his sister, who lived in Trappe. Now that he was going to be working in Trappe, it would make more sense to stay with his sister, but he told his mother he would decide later. Cordova and Trappe were located about 30 minutes apart, and the Choptank Inn was about midway between the two towns.

Link left his mother's house and drove to meet his friends at a home in Cordova. He ended up leaving his car in the parking lot of a butcher shop; it's unclear why he left his car here, but it seems likely he knew he was going to be drinking and thought it was safer to catch a ride with one of his friends. They arrived at the Choptank Inn less than 15 minutes later and spent the next few hours playing pool and drinking. Shortly before 2:00 am, Link ordered a final drink when the bartender announced that it was time for last call. He had been in good spirits all night, telling his friends all about his new caretaker position and how much he thought he was really going to enjoy the job.

Link quickly finished his last drink; it seems he may have finished it a little too quickly as shortly afterward he began to feel sick. He looked flushed as he told his friends that he was going to go outside and get some fresh air. He asked the friend who drove him to the Choptank Inn if he could borrow his car keys so he could sit in the car. His friend tossed him the keys and said he would be out as soon as he finished his last game of pool.

One of the patrons who was pulling out of the parking lot around that time recalled seeing Link standing next to a blue car in the lot; this was the last confirmed sighting of Link. When his friends walked out of the Choptank Inn just a few minutes later, there was no sign of Link. He had unlocked his friend's car and put the keys in the ignition, most likely so he could turn the radio on, but he wasn't with the car and he wasn't anywhere near the parking lot. Confused, his friends wondered if he had felt worse than he let on and had grabbed a ride with someone else so he could get home sooner.

They tried calling Link at his mother's house, but he wasn't there. Linda thought he might have gone to stay with his sister, but soon learned that she hadn't heard from him at all that night. Concerned, Linda called the Maryland State Police and reported her son missing, but police noted that he was an adult and free to come and go as he pleased.

Link's family and friends began searching the area for him and found his car in the butcher shop parking lot where Link had left it. Once his car was located, Linda called the Maryland State Police back and got them to take a missing person report. She had already been convinced that he hadn't disappeared voluntarily, and the fact that he was without his only form of transportation made the theory even less likely.

The Maryland State Police opened up a missing person investigation and began interviewing Link's friends and family. They started with the friends who had been with Link on the night he went missing, but they each told the same story without variation: They had all been drinking and playing pool, Link finished his last drink around 2:00 am, complained he felt sick and needed fresh air, and went outside with the keys to his friend's car. They had expected to find him waiting for them when the rest of the group made their way to the parking lot a few minutes later, but he had vanished.

Link was married at the time of his disappearance but was estranged from his wife and she was already dating someone else. Ironically, she was arrested two months after Link went missing; her boyfriend had committed a string of burglaries and she was charged as an accomplice. Detectives thoroughly looked into this but determined that it was not in any way connected to Link's disappearance.

Linda told police her son was a happy-go-lucky person who had been at a good place in life. He had started a new job and was very close with his mother and his sister, and had never been the type of person who would run away from his problems. He had a circle of close friends and no known enemies, and there was nothing in his past that suggested he would have any reason to disappear.

Detectives conducted a thorough background check on Link and could find nothing that would make him a target for foul play, but as time went on without any word from him, they began to believe that something had happened to him that night. Still, with absolutely no evidence to suggest otherwise, they hoped that he was still alive somewhere. His family couldn't believe that he would simply disappear and not contact them. Although they preferred to think he was still alive, they didn't think it was likely.

Linda was consumed by the desire to find her son. She spent weeks driving all over Talbot County, Maryland looking for anything that might lead her closer to Link. She hung up missing posters and distributed missing person flyers, and prayed that someone would call police and tell them what had happened to Link.

The case seemed to go cold almost immediately, and the family sometimes felt like they were the only people out there looking for Link. Months went by with absolutely no progress on the case, but Linda continued to travel around the area to put up posters and plead for help finding her son. She began to mark important dates, like Link's birthday and the first anniversary of his disappearance by tying ribbons on a tree in her front yard that the family had named "Link's Tree" years before.

When Link was a less-experienced driver, he had

accidentally run over the small tree and his family thought he had killed it. The tree survived, though, and over the years grew to be about 6 feet tall. Now, Linda carefully tied ribbons around the trunk and added white lights. It was a fitting tribute to Link.

Linda spent the first anniversary of her son's disappearance driving around and replacing old missing posters with fresh ones. She still thought about Link on a daily basis, and her heart would jump whenever the phone rang. She kept praying it would be Link, or at least news about him, but it never was.

By the time Link had been missing for three years, Linda had nearly lost all hope of seeing her son alive again. Although she wanted to think he was still alive, she was convinced that he had been killed, and she believed there were people in the area who knew exactly what had happened to Link. She felt frustrated, as she knew she would probably never learn Link's fate unless someone finally decided to come forward. The waiting was becoming unbearable.

In 1996, an unidentified male body was found not far from where Link was last seen. Linda was an emotional wreck when she learned that the victim was of the same approximate age, weight, and height as Link; she felt as if she could barely breathe until she finally got the call from police stating that the body was not that of her son. Although she desperately wanted Link to be found, part of her still wanted to believe that he was alive. Finding out that the victim wasn't Link allowed her to hold on to that hope.

Linda's hopes were raised in May 1999 when a man who had lived in Cordova reported seeing Link at a restaurant in Virginia Beach, Virginia. Although he didn't speak to him, he was so certain that it had been Link that

Linda decided to travel to Virginia and look for herself. She spent five days there, showing Link's picture to everyone she encountered. She spoke to the manager at the restaurant where the sighting had taken place, and the manager said that Link's photograph looked very familiar.

Linda walked up and down Virginia Beach's boardwalk, distributing missing person flyers and talking with local business owners, customers, tourists, and homeless people. Although several people thought that they recognized Link from the photographs Linda showed them, there were no definite sightings.

Discouraged, Linda went to the Virginia State Police armed with missing person flyers and posters, and they told her they would place them around the area and would keep an eye out for Link. They cautioned Linda that there was always a possibility that Link didn't want to be found. If they did locate him, and he didn't want anyone else to know where he was, they would have to honor his wishes. Linda was certain that wasn't the case but said she understood. She just wanted confirmation that he was alive.

There were a few more potential sightings of Link over the years, and Linda traveled all over Maryland, Virginia, and North Carolina following up on potential leads about her son. Eventually, the sightings stopped, and Linda struggled to keep the case in the public eye. For years, she continued to hang up missing posters and check in with detectives, but there was never anything new to report.

On the 15th anniversary of Link's disappearance, Linda added yet another ribbon to his tree. She said that deep down she knew he was dead, but she just wanted to know what had happened to him and be able to bring him home for a proper burial.

In 2016, Maryland State Police took yet another look at the case and made a public plea for information. They stated that they believed there were people who were close to Link at the time that likely know more than they have told police, and they hoped they would finally do the right thing and come forward so the family could have some measure of closure. They started to re-interview many of the people that were interviewed as part of the initial investigation, hoping that they might be able to pick up on some kind of clue that was missed earlier.

Linda spent the rest of her life searching tirelessly for answers about what had happened to her son but unfortunately died on March 8, 2019, without ever learning the truth.

The Maryland State Police have said since the beginning that there have been very few leads in the case, and they describe Link's disappearance as a huge mystery. They do believe that he encountered foul play, and was likely killed on the same night that he went missing. Although they still receive occasional tips, they have never been able to develop any solid leads or suspects. They still believe the case can be solved, but admit that it will likely require someone with knowledge of the case to finally come forward and tell them exactly what happened to Link that April night.

Robert John Bornos was just 25 years old when he went missing from Easton, Maryland in April 1993. He has brown eyes and brown hair, and at the time of his disappearance, he was 5 feet 8 inches tall and weighed 165 pounds. He was last seen wearing blue jeans, a t-shirt with "The Who" on the front, white socks, and orange and white sneakers. He had eyeglasses with brown plastic frames, his right ear was pierced, and he had a tattoo of a heart on his left arm. If you have any information about Robert, please contact the Maryland State Police at 410-290-0050 or 410-819-4747.

Diana Braungardt

Diana Braungardt, an 18-year-old senior in high school, was in a hurry to leave work on the evening of March 11, 1987. She worked part-time as a clerk at the Venture store in Crystal City, Missouri, and when her shift was over at 10:00 pm that Wednesday night she immediately punched out and headed for the parking lot. Diana told her coworkers that she wanted to go right home to study for a test she had to take the following day. Diana's home in Festus, Missouri was located just a few minutes away from the mall, but she never made it there.

Her parents, Marvin and Jane Braungardt, started to get concerned about Diana when she wasn't home by 10:30 pm. She was a responsible teenager, and would always call them if she were going to be late. They sat up for an hour, anxiously waiting to hear the sound of Diana coming up the front steps. When she didn't come home, Marvin drove to the Twin City Mall, where the Venture store was located.

It didn't take him long to locate the bright yellow 1982 Ford Escort Diana used to get back and forth from work; it was one of the few cars left in the mall parking lot. There was no sign of Diana in or around the car. The mall, which had closed more than an hour earlier, was dark and locked. Unsure what to do, Marvin drove home, and Jane started calling all of Diana's friends. Most of them were already asleep and confused about why she was calling them so late. None of them had seen Diana.

Although they tried to convince themselves that

Diana had planned to spend the night with a friend and simply forgotten to tell them, deep down her parents knew that wasn't the case. Diana had always been good about calling home, and there had never been a time when they didn't know where she was. When the sun rose and there was still no word from Diana, Marvin called the Crystal City Police Department and reported her missing.

Marvin was a pastor at the First United Methodist Church in Crystal City, and the family was well-respected in the community. Diana attended Festus High School, where she was a popular student who got good grades and was never in any kind of trouble. Marvin and Jane told police that their daughter did not currently have a boyfriend, and had recently started taking modeling classes on weekends. She had no problems at home or school, and she had no history of running away. They were certain that someone must have abducted the teenager.

Law enforcement initially thought that the 18-year-old might have decided to simply run off for a while. To their credit, though, they did launch an investigation right away. Detectives started calling Diana's friends and classmates before they left for school that morning, asking about Diana's mindset and if she had been having any trouble in her life. After speaking with those who knew her best, investigators were convinced that Diana was not the kind of teenager who would voluntarily leave home without telling anyone.

Investigators found nothing to indicate that Diana had any problems in life that would lead to her running away from home. She had gotten into an argument with her parents several weeks before; she left home and spent the night with a friend, but she told her parents where she was going, called her mother as soon as she got there, and told her that she would be home the following day. She returned by the time she promised, and she later told friends that she felt bad about the argument because her parents treated her like a queen.

Diana and her brother had both been adopted at birth, and detectives considered the possibility that Diana may have left to try and locate her birth parents. Marvin and Jane had previously offered to assist her in learning more about them, however, and she had declined. She considered Marvin and Jane to be her real parents.

Diana's car was searched thoroughly, but investigators found no signs of foul play in or around the car. They believed that Diana never made it to her car after leaving work the previous night, but had likely been abducted as she made her way to her car. None of her personal belongings that she normally carried were found in the car, and a check of all nearby trash cans and dumpsters failed to yield any relevant evidence. She had been carrying her purse and had been wearing a jacket she borrowed from her older brother; these items were never found.

Once Diana's disappearance was picked up by the news media, a woman called police to tell them that she believed she saw Diana on the night she disappeared. The woman had been driving past the Twin City Mall when she realized her baby needed a diaper change. She pulled into the mall parking lot and completed the diaper change, then tossed the dirty diaper into a dumpster. As she was leaving the parking lot, she saw a man speaking with a young woman who appeared to have just come out of the mall. The witness didn't pay much attention to the interaction at the time but later identified Diana as the young woman she had seen.

Some of Diana's co-workers noted that the last customer Diana had waited on before she left for the evening had appeared to linger around after he was finished checking out. They had assumed he was simply waiting for another customer who was still in the mall but now wondered if he might have had something to do with Diana's disappearance. They described the customer as a white man who was 5 feet 10 inches tall, between 35 and 40 years old, and clean-shaven with dark hair. He had a fairly dark complexion and had small bumps on his face. The description they gave was very similar to the description given by the woman who had stopped to change her baby's diaper.

Detectives released a sketch of the man and asked the public for help locating him. They said that he was not considered a suspect, but since he finished his shopping around the same time that Diana left the store, they hoped he might have witnessed something. Although they received a number of calls about the man, he remained unidentified.

A few days after Diana's disappearance, police received a call from a woman who had been driving on Interstate 55, located to the south of Festus, that Wednesday night. She told them she observed a young woman matching the missing girl's description standing up against a bridge rail on the highway. Police were unable to confirm the sighting.

Months went by, and both law enforcement and Diana's family were frustrated by the lack of progress on the case. Police had made numerous public appeals for information, but Diana seemed to vanish into thin air. They had been unsuccessful in identifying her last customer of the night, and no one else came forward to report seeing her after she left the store. While detectives still believed that they were dealing with a case of foul play, the fact that they had been unable to locate Diana's body gave her family some hope that she might still be alive.

Detectives heard many rumors about what might have happened to Diana, but few facts. Many tipsters called in claiming to have knowledge about the case, but when investigators followed up with them, their information would turn out to be third or fourth-hand. They would then try to track down the origin of the claim, only to find out it was simply a rumor started by someone with no involvement in the case. During the first two years of the investigation, they followed up on hundreds of these false leads, never finding any solid evidence about what had happened to Diana.

As time went by, Diana's family began to accept the fact that she was most likely not alive. They knew she hadn't run away; she had less than $20 with her when she vanished, and no access to credit cards. Her bank account remained untouched, and her Social Security number was never used. Still, they clung to the hope that she might have been held against her will and was now suffering from memory loss, and they continued to hang up missing person posters and hand out flyers. Whenever they traveled anywhere, they made sure to bring missing posters with them, carefully hanging them up in case Diana had made her way across the country.

The family held a prayer vigil for Diana on the fifth anniversary of her disappearance, and her mother told reporters that time had done nothing to ease the pain of her loss. The fact that there had never been any real leads in the case made it even more difficult to bear, as Diana's loved ones had no idea what might have happened to her. They could accept the fact that she was dead, but they still wanted to know how it had happened and where her body was located. More than anything, they just wanted to be able to bring her home.

It took Jane more than a decade before she was able to finally go through Diana's belongings and give away some of her clothing. She hung onto a few items that she couldn't bear to part with but admitted that she found it hard to look at Diana's things. It was painful for her to look at pictures of her daughter and think of all that could have been.

Law enforcement decided to take another look at Diana's case in 2004. Although they hadn't received any new leads in years, they thought taking a fresh look at the case might reveal something that was missed during the initial investigation. They were certain that Diana hadn't left voluntarily and that there was someone in the community who knew exactly what had happened to her. All the detectives who had worked on the case desperately wanted to be able to give Marvin and Jane some answers, and they were grateful to know that their daughter hadn't been forgotten.

Despite the new push to solve the case, detectives received few leads and the investigation soon stalled once again. They had nearly a dozen boxes of paperwork from interviews they had done, tips that were called in, and searches that had been conducted. They had invested thousands of hours on the case, but the only thing they knew for sure was that Diana was still missing, and they were certain it was due to foul play.

In 2007, detectives made some progress when they interviewed a man who resembled the composite sketch of the man seen talking to Diana on the evening she disappeared. He had lived in the area for decades, and by 2007 was in jail on unrelated charges. Although investigators had no evidence proving he was linked to Diana's disappearance, they stated that he hadn't given them any reason to clear him as a suspect. He is currently serving a life sentence in a Missouri state prison and has never been charged in connection with Diana's case.

Marvin and Jane never gave up their search for Diana, though they knew that they were looking for a body. Unfortunately, Marvin died in 2015 and Jane died in 2017; Diana was listed in each obituary as dying before them. Her brother is still alive, however, and she still has many friends in the Festus area who would like to see justice in her case.

Diana Jane Braungardt was just 18 years old when she went missing from Crystal City, Missouri in March 1987. She was a senior in high school and told co-workers that she planned to go home and study when her shift was over, but she never made it home and detectives believe she was a victim of foul play. Diana has hazel eyes and dark blonde hair, and at the time of her disappearance, she was 5 feet 6 inches tall and weighed 108 pounds. She was last seen wearing turquoise pants, a white shirt with a colorful print, her work smock, a black coat, and brown loafers. If you have any information about Diana, please contact the Crystal City Police Department at 314-937-4601.

Lynn Burdick

Lynn Burdick just wanted to save up enough money for a prom dress. Although the high school senior was shy around boys and did not expect to have a date, she wanted to go to the prom anyway. Her family's finances were tight at the time – her mother had emphysema and her health had been declining – so Lynn increased the number of hours she worked at her cousin's convenience store, the Barefoot Peddler Country Store, located in the tiny town of Florida, Massachusetts. She was alone there on the evening of Saturday, April 17, 1982; normally her best friend worked alongside her but she was away that weekend. The store was located only a few hundred yards from her home, though, and she never felt unsafe.

Suzanne Burdick was Lynn's cousin; she was also a co-owner of the store. Although the area was extremely safe, she didn't like the idea of a teenager working alone at night, and would often stop by the store to check on Lynn. On this particular evening, however, one of her young children was sick in bed with the flu and Suzanne needed to stay at home and take care of her. She phoned the store around 8:00 pm to see how Lynn was doing, and the two chatted for a few minutes. Lynn told Suzanne that the rainy night seemed to be keeping customers away; it had been a very slow night with no problems. Her job mostly entailed sitting at the counter until a customer came in, then she would ring them up for their beer, groceries, and other small items.

While the two cousins were talking, Suzanne heard

the jingling sound of a bell which indicated that the store's front door had just been opened. Lynn told her that a customer had just come in, and got off the phone so she could wait on him. She promised to call Suzanne back once she closed the convenience store for the night at 9:00 pm.

Around 8:40 pm, another customer entered the store and was surprised to find that there was no one inside. He could see an open paperback book on the checkout counter along with a half-finished soft drink, but there didn't appear to be any employees in the small store. He knew Lynn's family and was aware that the teenager normally worked there on Saturday nights; when she didn't appear after a couple of minutes he called the family home and let them know that there was no one at the store. The Burdick family immediately called the police.

A trooper from the Massachusetts State Police arrived at the Barefoot Peddler and examined the scene. There was nothing to indicate that a struggle had taken place inside the small store; everything was neat and tidy, and there were several displays close to the counter that appeared to be undisturbed. There was $187 missing from the cash register, leading them to believe that a robbery may have occurred. They concluded that whoever robbed the place was unaware that cashiers would routinely place money underneath the counter so that the register never had more than a couple of hundred dollars in it; police found this cache of money untouched.

Lynn had been reading a book between customers, and it remained on the counter along with her soda. Her jacket and purse were missing. This would lead to some initial speculation that Lynn had taken the money herself and run off, but detectives soon determined this was not a viable theory. Lynn did not have a car or driver's license, her best friend was out of town, and she didn't have a boyfriend. She also would have been aware of the money that was underneath the counter; if she were going to run off, she likely would have taken this as well.

Lynn, who had turned 18 a few months earlier, was a senior at McCann Vocational Technical High School and just weeks away from graduation. She was a shy and quiet teenager, known for being studious and well-behaved. When she wasn't at school or the Barefoot Peddler, she was usually at home helping to take care of her ill mother or doing volunteer work for people with disabilities. She volunteered with several charities in the Berkshire area; the day after she disappeared she had been scheduled to participate in a benefit at a local roller-skating rink to raise money for people with cerebral palsy. She was a genuinely nice teenager who enjoyed helping those who were less fortunate than her.

Lynn lived in a small, unpainted clapboard house located close to the Barefoot Peddler. It was somewhat crowded; she lived there with her mother, father, aunt, uncle, and two cousins. Lynn had her own small bedroom located in the attic of the home; it was always kept tidy and contained many of her childhood toys.

While some may have found her life in the Berkshires to be somewhat boring, Lynn seemed to be happy and certainly never complained. She was quiet around most people but was more open with a few close friends, and they said she was funny and a joy to be around. She didn't smoke, drink, or do drugs, despite having easy access to cigarettes and beer as both were sold at the Barefoot Peddler.

Although Lynn had dreamed of one day going to college, she knew that it was financially impossible at the time. She planned to remain at home after her high school graduation to help take care of her mother. While doing so, she hoped to save up some money so that she could eventually realize her dream of getting a college education.

Detectives were confident that Lynn was not the kind of teenager who would steal money from her cousin's store and take off for the unknown. They were convinced that she had been abducted during a robbery; they estimated that the crime had taken place shortly after she had gotten off the phone with her cousin around 8:10 pm. Her mother reported that she had called the store at 8:30 pm and not gotten an answer; she hadn't been too concerned at the time as she assumed that Lynn was helping a customer. Detectives believed that Lynn had already been abducted at that point.

The Barefoot Peddler was located on the corner of Central Shaft Road and Route 2 in Florida, Massachusetts. The tiny town – home to approximately 700 people – was located along the Mohawk Trail in the foothills of the Green Mountain Range. Due to its isolated location, crime, in general, was rare and abductions were even rarer. It wasn't the sort of place that people would randomly drive through, leading police to speculate that the abductor was familiar with the area.

On the same evening that Lynn had disappeared, a woman attending Williams College reported that an unidentified man had tried to abduct her from campus. She managed to escape from him as he tried to force her into his vehicle around 7:00 pm; although she had some bruises she was relatively unscathed and able to describe the attacker to police.

After police learned of the attempted abduction, a police officer recalled that he had seen a similar vehicle traveling on Route 2 in the direction of Florida, located just

8 miles away. Since he had been unaware of the attempted abduction at the time, he hadn't pursued the vehicle. Now police worried that the man had continued along Route 2, which would have taken him directly to the Barefoot Peddler. Unfortunately, they were never able to locate the man or his vehicle.

On Sunday, police, firefighters, and local residents conducted a large-scale search for Lynn, scouring the mountainous terrain for any clues as to what might have happened to her. It was hard work, as rain and snow had combined to cover the area in a layer of mud and frozen slush. They combed through dirt roads and searched through abandoned sheds and other buildings, but were unable to find anything relevant to the investigation.

Over the next ten days, hundreds of people took part in the search for Lynn. The terrain was rough and included steep ravines, creeks, and heavily wooded areas. There were numerous decaying cabins that had long been abandoned by their owners, desolate dirt roads, and a few scattered campgrounds. The entire area was thoroughly searched, but nothing was found.

Authorities scoured the Hoosac Tunnel that had been bored through the Hoosac Range of the Green Mountains; at almost 5 miles in length, it was considered one of the greatest engineering feats of the 19th Century. It ran from the town of Florida to North Adams, Massachusetts, and searchers covered it completely. Once again, their search ended without finding anything that helped lead them to Lynn.

Lynn's father, Rufus Burdick, took time off from his job as a machinist to assist in the search for his daughter. Even after the official search was called off on April 27th, he refused to stop looking for her. He was convinced that she had been abducted and was being held somewhere against her will; he wouldn't even consider the fact that she might be dead and searched tirelessly for her. Eventually, the family's precarious financial situation forced him to return to work, but he never stopped believing Lynn would be found alive.

Years went by, and though police received a few sporadic tips about the case, they made no progress in finding Lynn. They followed up on each lead they developed, but all led to dead ends. In 1995, Rufus received an anonymous letter in the mail from someone claiming to have information about Lynn. They stated that she had been abducted and killed by a man who lived in North Adams, but declined to give any further clues about where her body might be found. Police were familiar with the name of the person being accused of the crime, and they interviewed him extensively but were never able to link him to the robbery or Lynn's disappearance.

The 1995 letter provided the last significant lead in the case, and though Lynn's family and authorities both made public appeals for the writer of the letter to get back in contact with them, the person never reached out to them again. Despite the length of time that has passed, police believe that Lynn's case can still be solved if the right person will finally come forward to tell detectives all that they know about the case.

Lynn Burdick was just 18 years old when she went missing from Florida, Massachusetts in April 1982. She has blue eyes and brown hair, and at the time of her disappearance, she was 5 feet 4 inches tall and weighed 115 pounds. It is unknown what clothing she was wearing when she was last seen, but she had her McCann Technical Vocational High School jacket with her and was wearing her high school class ring; this ring had a blue stone and was engraved with either her initials or her full name. If you have any information about Lynn, please contact the Massachusetts State Police at 413-499-1112.

Susan Wolff Cappel

Susan Wolff Cappel was in a good mood when she went to work on the afternoon of Tuesday, March 16, 1982. The 19-year-old was in the process of getting a divorce, and her estranged husband had been granted temporary custody of Damin, their 18-month-old son. Before she left for her 4:00 pm shift in the deli department of the Newcomerstown, Ohio IGA supermarket, she learned that a custody hearing had finally been scheduled. She had been ecstatic to receive this news, as she was certain that she would be granted custody of Damin. She told her mother that she could finally see a light at the end of the tunnel, and she was looking forward to the future.

Susan and Allen Cappel had been high school sweethearts. They got married in February of 1980, while Susan was still a senior in high school; Damin was born later that same year. The couple found an apartment near Bolivar, Ohio, about a half-hour away from Susan's childhood home in Newcomerstown. Although they appeared to have a great marriage at first, it would only last about 23 months.

Allen, who worked for the Ohio Department of Transportation, had filed for divorce in January of 1982. Susan, who had been a homemaker, was unsure how she was going to support herself; because of this, Allen had been given temporary custody of Damin. He remained in the apartment the couple had shared, leaving Susan to find her own place to live.

Susan had gone to her parents, James and Judy

41

Wolff, and asked them if they knew how she could go about getting welfare from the state. Her parents had been against the idea and told Susan they were more than willing to provide her with food and shelter until she got back on her feet. Susan had gratefully accepted their offer and immediately started trying to find a job so she could help with expenses. It didn't take her long; within weeks, she had a part-time job at IGA. She soon found a second job working two nights a week at a hospital in Canton, Ohio. They were impressed with her work and planned to make her a full-time employee once they finished an expansion project that was in progress.

Susan was working hard to get her life back together, and things were finally starting to improve. The only dark cloud that remained was the fact that Allen currently controlled when Susan was able to see her son. Susan had a planned visitation with Damin two days earlier, but at the last minute Allen had refused to allow her to see the child. Susan had been both angry and upset and had called her lawyer to complain about it the following day. He had called her back with the news that, after being delayed twice, a new date had finally been set for the long-awaited custody hearing.

Susan was thrilled at the thought that she might soon be reunited with her son, and she set about redecorating her childhood bedroom so he would have a place to stay. She bought him a new crib and picked out a pale green paint that she thought would look nice on the walls. She planned to spend the next day she had off from work painting.

Allen had retained possession of the only vehicle the couple had owned, so Susan was left without transportation. Her parents had been letting her use one of their cars to get back and forth to work, and Susan climbed into the car Tuesday afternoon to make the short drive to IGA. She pulled into the parking lot with plenty of time to spare before her 4:00 pm shift started, and happily made her way into the supermarket. She arrived at work carrying only her IGA vest; she had forgotten to grab her purse and wallet before she left the house but wasn't too concerned. She was only scheduled to work for five hours, and she didn't expect to need anything from her purse while she was there.

Susan's shift in the deli department that night was completely routine and uneventful. Her father had stopped in around 6:00 pm to pick up some items for dinner, and he noted that Susan was still in a good mood at that time. She mentioned that she planned to go right home after her shift was over at 9:00 pm, and he told her that he would see her then.

The rest of the evening passed by quickly, and Susan punched out right at 9:00 pm. One of her co-workers left around the same time, and as she stepped out into the parking lot she saw Susan making her way towards her car. Before she got there, another car pulled up in front of her, and Susan spoke briefly to the driver. She then walked around and got into the passenger seat of the car, which then drove out of the parking lot.

When Susan hadn't returned to her parents' house by 9:30 pm, they assumed that she had been asked to work late. As more time passed, they wondered if perhaps the teenager had decided to go out with some friends. Although she would normally call if she were going to be late, her parents knew that she had been under a great deal of stress because of the divorce; it was possible she had simply forgot to phone them. By midnight, they were growing increasingly concerned. They didn't want to overreact – Susan was an adult, and free to go out for the night if she wanted – but they couldn't shake the feeling that something was wrong.

James and Judy spent a sleepless night waiting to hear the sound of Susan pulling into the driveway, but the street was silent. By morning, they were in a state of panic; they called the police at 9:21 am and reported their daughter missing. The Newcomerstown Police saw no need to immediately look into Susan's disappearance. Instead, they assured her parents that she had most likely decided that she needed to get away from everything for a while. After all, she had been under a lot of stress recently.

Susan's parents acknowledged that Susan had been going through a lot, but were adamant that she would not disappear voluntarily. She had been looking forward to the upcoming custody hearing, and the divorce finally seemed to be winding down. She never would have left without letting someone know where she was going to be just in case something happened to her son.

James drove to the IGA where he had last seen his daughter and was disturbed to find her car still parked in the parking lot, in the same spot where it had been when he stopped by the market the previous night. After alerting Newcomerstown Police that he had located her car, they gave him permission to drive it home.

After speaking with some of the employees at IGA, Susan's parents learned that one of their daughter's co-workers had seen her getting into an unknown car after her shift was over. The co-worker hadn't thought much of it at the time and was unable to provide any details about the driver of the car. She described the car as an older, light blue car that had a good deal of rust on it.

Once they heard about the blue car, James and Judy immediately suspected that Susan's estranged husband was somehow involved in her disappearance. He had a friend named Rick who owned an older model Plymouth Satellite that was blue in color, and they wondered if this was the car Susan's co-worker had seen.

After learning that Susan had left behind her purse, identification, two uncashed paychecks, and all other personal belongings, police started to take a serious look at her disappearance. Although they still weren't convinced that foul play was involved, they did open an investigation and started to question Susan's family, friends, and co-workers.

James and Judy told police their hunch that Allen and his friend might have been involved, and detectives interviewed Allen. He adamantly denied that he had anything at all to do with Susan's disappearance, and scoffed at the thought that he had enlisted his friend Rick to do anything. Allen told investigators that he believed Susan had gone off on her own and would return at some point when she was ready.

Unfortunately, two weeks after Susan went missing, Rick and his cousin were killed in a car accident while Rick was driving the Plymouth. Detectives were never able to question them, and they were never able to confirm if the car Susan got into was a Plymouth Satellite. Her co-worker underwent hypnosis to see if she could recall any other details about the car, but she was unable to remember anything useful.

James and Judy continued searching for their daughter, but the official investigation into Susan's disappearance was relatively superficial. Since they still thought there was a chance that Susan had left voluntarily, they never conducted any physical searches for her and did little other than interview those people who knew her. There were several reported sightings of Susan during the first couple of years after she went missing, and this seemed to confirm law enforcement's suspicions that she was still alive.

About a month after Susan's disappearance, the younger sister of one of her friends claimed that she saw Susan sitting in a blue car with Allen Cappel. She told police that Susan had permed her hair; prior to her disappearance, she had always worn her hair long and feathered in the front. Since the girl who reported seeing Susan was quite familiar with her, police believed it was a credible sighting. Allen, however, denied seeing or hearing from Susan after she went missing.

A year after her disappearance, a Greyhound bus driver reported seeing Susan on a bus in Ohio. According to him, she had purchased a ticket to travel from Reno, Nevada to Newcomerstown, Ohio, and was carrying only a small bag. She had asked him if she could be let off the bus at a gas station in Newcomerstown, but the driver told her that passengers were only allowed to be let off the bus once it reached the Greyhound station.

The woman got off the bus at the station, but as soon as she left the bus, she started running towards the gas station. The driver saw a missing poster for Susan at the station and called police to report that he believed she had just been on his bus. Police responded immediately and conducted an extensive search of the area, but found no sign of Susan. It is unknown if the woman on the bus was actually Susan or if the sighting was a case of mistaken identity.

In an effort to keep the case in the public eye, James and Judy designed "Missing Mother" flyers with several pictures of Susan on them, and they distributed them throughout the area. They also offered a $500 reward for any information about Susan's whereabouts, but no one seemed to know where the teenager might be.

When the flyers failed to help locate their daughter, James and Judy hired a private investigator. They were also interviewed on several local television news programs, and they appealed to the public for help in finding out what happened to Susan. Despite an exhaustive search that took them from New Jersey to California, they were unable to find any clues pertaining to Susan's fate.

The Tuscarawas County Sheriff's Office is the lead agency in charge of Susan's case, and they have investigated all tips and leads that have come in over the years, but admit that they still have no idea what happened to Susan. The fact that so much time has passed without any contact from her leads them to believe that foul play likely took place, but they still have no evidence to support this theory.

Damin was forced to grow up without his mother; James and Judy attempted to sue Allen for custody of the child shortly after Susan's disappearance and later launched an active campaign to increase grandparents' rights in the state of Ohio.

Allen was granted a divorce in 1983 after Susan had been missing for one year; he got remarried five months later. He always maintained that he had nothing to do with Susan's disappearance, and detectives never found any evidence to substantiate the theory that he was involved. He was killed in a car accident in 2003.

James and Judy had Susan declared dead on February 3, 2015, nearly 33 years after she went to work and never returned home. Although they believe she was likely killed shortly after she left work that Tuesday night in 1982, they had never felt ready to have a formal declaration of death. They finally did so only because they wanted to hold a formal memorial service and erect a tombstone for her. The declaration didn't bring them any closure, and they still hope to learn what happened to their daughter.

Susan Wolff Cappel was just 19 years old when she went missing from Newcomerstown, Ohio in March 1982. She has brown eyes and brown hair, and at the time of her disappearance, she was 5 feet 4 inches tall and weighed 107 pounds. She was last seen wearing a white and brown striped turtleneck sweater, brown corduroy jeans, a red IGA smock, and reddish-brown oxfords. Her upper left front tooth was discolored and she has a scar on the upper right side of her lip. She had previously fractured her nose in a car accident. If you have any information about Susan, please contact the Tuscarawas County Sheriff's Office at 330-339-2000 or the Newcomerstown Police Department at 740-498-6161.

Brenda Condon

Brenda Condon arrived early for her bartending shift at Carl's Bad Tavern in Spring Township, PA on the evening of February 26, 1991. She parked her 1986 Mercury Capri in the parking lot and noted with satisfaction that she still had 15 minutes before she was scheduled to begin work. She had only recently started working at Carl's Bad Tavern – this was her third shift- but she had been a patron there before she was hired, and she knew the clientele well. Most of the tavern's customers were regulars, and she was looking forward to spending the evening chatting with them.

It was a bitterly cold Tuesday night, and the bar wasn't very crowded. There were a few customers that Brenda had never seen before, but for the most part, she was familiar with everyone. She kept herself busy making small talk with patrons and serving drinks, and the hours flew by. The bar was nearly empty when she announced that it was time for last call, and the few remaining customers slowly filtered out into the frosty winter air. By 1:15 am, the bar was empty and Brenda began going through her closing checklist.

Brenda cleaned up the bar area and made sure all the alcohol bottles were placed neatly on their assigned shelf. She totaled the bar's receipts and put away the deposit so it could be taken to the bank the next day. With her side work finished, all Brenda had left to do was turn off the lights and lock up. Once she did that, she could head home to State College, PA. She never made it. At some point after she finished cleaning up, Brenda disappeared, never to be seen again.

The following morning, a vendor showed up to restock the cigarette machine located inside the bar. Although it was still early, he noticed a car in the parking lot and found the front door to the bar was unlocked. He didn't notice anything unusual inside, despite the fact that he didn't see any employees. He simply restocked the machine and left. As an independent contractor, he rarely interacted with employees at any of the businesses where his cigarette machines were located; his routine was to collect the money out of the machine and restock it with fresh products. He was in and out within minutes.

Day shift employees showed up at the tavern shortly after the cigarette vendor left, and they noticed that Brenda's Capri was still in the parking lot. They thought something was wrong when they found the front door was unlocked, but when they went inside nothing appeared to be out of place. The bar was neat and clean, and all the money from the night before was right where it was supposed to be. In the men's room, however, they found the boots that Brenda had worn to work the previous night. They had been placed neatly next to the restroom door. After making a couple of phone calls and learning that Brenda had never arrived home the night before, they called the police.

Police were unable to find any signs of foul play inside the bar. Tables and chairs were still neatly arranged, and there were no broken bottles or glasses. There were no signs of robbery; all the money was accounted for and there was no alcohol missing. If a crime had taken place, it appeared that Brenda had been the sole target.

Detectives were confused about the placement of Brenda's boots; to their trained eyes, the scene appeared to be staged. Whoever had placed the boots there wanted them to be found, but there was no way of knowing who put them there. None of Brenda's other belongings were found in the tavern, and after checking her car investigators determined that Brenda's purse and keys were missing. Assuming that Brenda had decided to simply disappear for a while, police did no further investigating for the next few days.

Police were forced to re-evaluate their initial assumptions about Brenda's disappearance on March 2, 1991, when they learned that she had missed a scheduled visitation with her children. She had never done so in the past, and her family insisted that she would never go away without telling them.

Originally from Clearfield County, PA, Brenda had graduated from high school there in 1980 and married almost immediately afterward. She and her husband had two children, but their marriage eventually fell apart and Brenda moved to Williamsport, PA. The children remained with their father so they wouldn't have to switch schools, but he and Brenda maintained a friendly relationship and he allowed her to see the kids whenever she wanted.

Brenda's own mother died when she was just a toddler, so she knew how hard it could be for a child to be raised without a mother. She had recently moved to State College specifically so she could be closer to her children, and always looked forward to spending time with them. Everyone who knew her said the same thing: she would never voluntarily walk away from her kids.

In addition to her part-time bartending job, Brenda managed two cleaning services, one in Williamsport and one in State College. She was known for being very dependable, and it was completely out of her character to miss any time at work without letting someone know.

After learning more about Brenda's background, detectives decided to take a harder look at her case. They began interviewing anyone who had been in contact with her in the days leading up to her disappearance. They were able to quickly eliminate her ex-husband as a suspect and focused next on the other man in her life, boyfriend Gregory Palazzari.

Brenda and Greg had been dating for about two years, and she had been living with him in State College for about four months at the time of her disappearance. Greg told detectives that they had a very good relationship, and Brenda seemed to be very happy with the way her life was going. He agreed with Brenda's family that she would never leave on her own and was convinced that someone had abducted her.

Greg last spoke to Brenda shortly before she went to work that Tuesday; she had been in good spirits at the time, talking about what she wanted to do for her birthday the following weekend. She gave no indication that there was anything wrong, and she had never mentioned being afraid of anything.

Investigators launched an extensive physical search for Brenda on March 3, 1991, using tracking dogs, helicopters, and volunteers to assist in combing through the area surrounding the tavern. Unfortunately, in the time that passed between Brenda's disappearance and the start of the search, there had been a significant amount of snow in the area. They were unable to find any clues to Brenda's whereabouts.

After speaking with some of the customers who had been in the bar on the night Brenda disappeared, detectives were able to identify nearly all the patrons who stopped by the tavern during her shift. Most of the people had been local to the area, regulars who stopped in just about every evening either to socialize after work or for a late-night drink. There were only three people in the bar that night who were not part of the regular crowd, and police released descriptions of these men and the clothes they were wearing hoping that someone would recognize them. They stressed that none of the men were suspects, but were wanted for questioning simply because they may have witnessed something.

Regular customers noticed that Brenda had been her normal cheerful self that night, and had spent time chatting with each customer. Like all good bartenders, she had a way of making people feel comfortable. They noticed that one man in particular seemed to be sticking around to speak with Brenda when it was getting close to last call. At the time, they hadn't seen his behavior as suspicious. Brenda had a very approachable personality, and she was always willing to strike up a conversation with a stranger. Now, regular patrons wondered if this man might have had something to do with Brenda's disappearance. With only a vague description to go on, however, detectives were never able to identify this man.

Greg told detectives that he believed Brenda's disappearance had something to do with her job at the bar. He was afraid that one of the patrons might have been a little too interested in Brenda and had attacked her when she declined his advances. Investigators looked into this theory, and admit it is a viable one, but they have never been able to develop any solid information to confirm it.

Carl's Bad Tavern was located very close to a major interstate, and was occasionally patronized by people who were just driving through the area and wanted to stop for a drink. If Brenda had been abducted by a transient, she could have been taken just about anywhere in the country.

Recognizing this, detectives did what they could to send her missing person flyer to various agencies nationwide, but received few leads.

Weeks went by with no progress on the case, and it slowly went cold. Detectives interviewed more than 100 people during the course of their investigation, and administered six or seven polygraph examinations. They were never able to develop any solid suspects, and each detective has their own theory about who they believe might be responsible.

Brenda's sister, Iris, has believed from the beginning that her sister's disappearance was somehow linked to Greg's activities; at the time, he was rumored to be a drug dealer. She worried that Brenda had seen or heard something that she wasn't supposed to, a secret that someone was willing to kill over. Greg denied these accusations and insisted he had nothing to do with his girlfriend's disappearance, and detectives agreed. They stated that there has never been anything pointing to Greg's involvement.

While the rumor about Greg's involvement in Brenda's disappearance might not have been true, the rumor that he was a drug dealer was, but it would take investigators years to prove it. In 2009, he was arrested for dealing cocaine. According to detectives, he was bringing in around $50,000 a month, and they believed he had been doing so for years. Even after this arrest, however, they still do not believe he had anything to do with Brenda's case.

Brenda's family has never stopped searching for her, though they have long since come to terms with the fact that they are almost certainly looking for a body. Brenda's kids are adults now, and Brenda, wherever she is, is a grandmother. Her family believes that there are people who know what happened to Brenda on that cold February night, and they are hoping they will come forward with this information so they can finally give Brenda a proper burial.

Brenda Condon was 28 years old when she vanished from Spring Township, Pennsylvania in February 1991. She has blue eyes and reddish-brown hair, and at the time of her disappearance, she was 5 feet 4 inches tall and weighed 110 pounds. She was last seen wearing jeans and a black tank top with a silver shirt over top of the black one. She has a ring of roses tattooed on her right ankle, and she normally wore green-tinted contact lenses. If you have any information about Brenda, please contact the Pennsylvania State Police - Rockview Station at 814-355-7345.

Jennifer Fay

Jennifer Fay was aggravated on the evening of
November 14, 1989. The 16-year-old had been invited to a
party being held around the corner from her Brockton,
Massachusetts home, and she wanted to go. Instead, she
was stuck babysitting for her younger brother and sister.
She usually didn't mind babysitting for them, but she had
put up a fight about it on this particular evening. Her
mother, Dottie MacLean, held firm. She had already made
plans to go out with some of her friends that night and
told her oldest daughter that she was just going to have to
miss the party.

Although Jen seemed to give in, in reality, she was
just biding her time until her mother left. Once she was
sure Dottie was gone, she called her cousin, Tammy
Young. Tammy lived right around the corner, and she
agreed to come over and watch Jen's younger siblings so
the teenager could go out with her friends. As soon as
Tammy arrived, Jen breezed out the door of the Emerson
Avenue apartment, promising to be back before her
mother returned.

The party was being held just a few blocks away,
and it had been in full swing for a couple of hours before
Jen arrived. Shortly after she got there, she left with a
male acquaintance to get more alcohol from Rice's
Market, a local convenience store. Jen waited outside
while the male, who was 21 years old, went inside for
beer. The store was located at the end of Jen's street, so
she decided to stop by her apartment for a jacket on the

way back to the party. Once she grabbed her coat, she and the male started to walk back to Broad Place, where the party was located. Along the way, however, the male Jen was with got sick.

The 21-year-old had already been drinking for hours, and it apparently caught up with him on the walk back to the party. A witness reported seeing him vomiting on the side of the road; Jen was still with him at the time but she was talking to someone in a brown pickup truck who had pulled over alongside of her. By the time her acquaintance had finished being sick, Jen had walked over to the truck and climbed inside. She was never seen again.

Later that evening, Dottie called home to check up on her children; she expected Jen to answer the phone and was quite surprised when Tammy picked up instead. Tammy explained that she had come over to watch the children so Jen could go out, and Dottie was torn between anger and concern. She immediately cut her night short and returned home.

Dottie spent a sleepless night waiting for Jen to return home. There was still no sign of the teenager when the sun came up, so Dottie called the Brockton Police Department and reported her daughter missing.

Police immediately assumed that Jen had run away – she had done so in the past, though she always stayed in touch with her parents – and did not conduct any searches for her. Dottie was certain that Jen had not left home voluntarily, as she had not taken any of her belongings with her. Realizing that she wasn't going to get any help from police, she decided to launch her own investigation.

Dottie went door-to-door throughout the neighborhood, trying to find anyone who had seen Jen on the night she disappeared. For the most part, people seemed to avoid talking about it, which was a red flag to

Dottie. She also found it odd that none of Jen's friends who had been with her at the party ever called the house to see if Dottie had heard from Jen. She was convinced that they knew more than they were telling her, but there was little she could do to make them talk. Police remained uninterested in the case, convinced that Jen was just another teenage runaway.

It took three years before police finally assigned a detective to the case – three years of frustration and heartbreak for Dottie, who had insisted from the beginning that Jen was not a runaway. In 1992, detectives finally seemed to reach the same conclusion and admitted that it had been a mistake to assume Jen had disappeared voluntarily. They now believed that she had been abducted and most likely murdered, but found that all potential witnesses were completely uncooperative and refused to speak with investigators.

Detectives learned that many of the people Jen had been friends with at the time of her disappearance were involved with drugs and possibly other illegal activities, which was likely why most of them wouldn't cooperate. While police – and Dottie – believed that Jen's friends likely knew exactly what had happened the night the teenager disappeared, they all denied having any knowledge about the case.

Dottie described her daughter as being funny and outgoing, but also a bit naïve. She tended to trust people without question, and her mother now worried that this trait had gotten her into trouble. Jen had started hanging out with a different crowd not too long before she went missing. She loved to socialize and go to parties with her new friends, but she had chosen the wrong group of people to trust.

Although Dottie felt vindicated once detectives

admitted that they didn't believe Jen ran away from home, their admission did little to help find Jen. Between those who had been at the party refusing to talk to police and no witnesses coming forward with any new information, the case soon stalled and went cold.

Dottie did everything she could to make sure that people remembered that Jen was still missing, but it was an uphill battle. Jen's disappearance received no media attention at all for the first decade she was missing. The first reporter to take an interest in the case contacted Dottie in 1999, long after the investigation had gone cold.

In 2000, 16-year-old Molly Bish disappeared from her lifeguard job in Warren, Massachusetts, about 90 minutes away from Brockton. The case made national news, a fact that frustrated Dottie. She didn't begrudge the Bish family the attention they received, but she didn't understand why no one seemed to care about her daughter.

Molly's family would gain some measure of closure when her remains were found in 2003, but her murder remains unsolved. After her death, her family started the Molly Bish Foundation, and they funded several private investigators to work on Jen's case. These investigators would work alongside police trying to penetrate the wall of silence that surrounded Jen's disappearance.

In 2003, police received an anonymous tip that Jen had been murdered, and her body had been placed inside a truck which was then submerged in a Brockton pond. The pond, located just a few minutes from Jen's home, was thoroughly searched. Investigators found nothing to indicate a truck – or a body – had ever been placed there.

By 2005, with the help of private investigators, the search for Jen was renewed. They conducted several searches in different areas of Massachusetts, hoping to find something that might lead them closer to finding Jen. They combed through wooded areas, ponds, and fields; several private properties were also searched with consent from the owners. Nothing related to Jen's disappearance was located.

Private investigators managed to speak with over 120 people who had known Jen or had mutual friends with her; the fact that they were not part of local law enforcement seemed to work to their advantage and they had an easier time getting people to open up to them than Brockton detectives. They managed to track down the male who had gone to the convenience store with Jen shortly before she disappeared; he was living in Vermont, and though he had been reluctant to speak with police, he agreed to meet with private investigators. He told them that he had gone with Jen to her apartment so she could pick up a jacket, and they were headed back to the party when the man started feeling sick.

The man was able to confirm that Jen was last seen speaking with someone in a brown pickup truck, though he wasn't sure if there were one or two people inside. It is believed that whoever was in this truck was the last person to see Jen, and most likely played a part in her disappearance.

In May 2008, investigators searched through a secluded pond located in Avon, Massachusetts, just a few miles away from Brockton. Detectives had received a tip that Jen and her friends would sometimes throw parties at the pond, as it was isolated enough that they could hide from their parents and area law enforcement. Although no one was suggesting Jen had been buried there, investigators decided to search through the area anyway. They found nothing.

As years went by, Dottie grew more desperate to

learn what had happened to her daughter. She reached the point where she no longer cared who was responsible for Jen's disappearance; she just wanted her daughter back. Closure became more important than holding someone accountable for what they did, and she pleaded for anyone with information to please come forward. Her pleas fell on deaf ears.

Detectives have continued to plug away at the case over the years, and they believe they know what happened to Jen, but they lack the evidence to prove it. Private investigators have interviewed nearly 300 people, almost all of them teenagers when Jen went missing. Although none of them have admitted to any actual knowledge of what went on that night, investigators believe that Jen knew the person driving the brown truck seen near the party, and she got into it because she believed she could trust the driver.

They believe this man was responsible for killing her, though they don't think it was something that was planned ahead of time. There were two brown pickup trucks that belonged to young men in the Brockton neighborhood at that time. One of these pickup trucks went missing shortly after Jen's disappearance. There is no record of it being sold and it has never been re-registered, despite the fact that it was only three or four years old at the time. Although they have no direct evidence to link this to Jen, detectives believe it may be the key to cracking the case. They hope that someone with knowledge of what took place will finally come forward with the remaining pieces of the puzzle so Jen's case can be resolved.

In 2018, the mayor of Brockton announced that the city was going to name a recently renovated playground in McKinley Park after Jen. He hoped that it would give

Dottie a place where she could go to be with her daughter despite the fact that her body has never been found. While they certainly appreciate the gesture, Jen's family would love nothing more than to finally be able to bring her home.

Jennifer Fay was just 16 years old when she went missing from Brockton, Massachusetts in November 1989. She has blue eyes and blonde hair, and at the time of her disappearance, she was 5 feet 4 inches tall and weighed approximately 95 pounds. She was last seen wearing blue jeans, a purple shirt, white sneakers, and a black silk jacket with an Iron Maiden patch on it. If you have any information about Jen, please contact the Brockton Police Department at 508-941-0200.

Darla Harper

Darla Harper spent the evening of March 4, 1986, chatting with a neighbor who had stopped by to visit her at her Gravel Ridge, Arkansas apartment. The neighbor left around 9:30 pm, leaving 25-year-old Darla and her young daughter, Leslie, alone in the small apartment. What happened after the neighbor left remains a mystery; Darla was never seen again.

Darla, a 1977 graduate of Pine Bluff High School, worked as a personnel analyst in the Little Rock office of the Internal Revenue Service. When she failed to show up for work the following morning, her manager was immediately concerned. Darla was an extremely reliable and responsible employee; in her four years working for the IRS, she had never missed work without calling to let someone know first. When phone calls to her apartment went unanswered, one of her co-workers was dispatched to go check on her.

Darla was not at her apartment when her co-worker arrived; he found her front door open and her 2-year-old daughter inside. Leslie was alone and confused but unharmed. Although there were no signs of a struggle inside the apartment, there was blood on the outside of Darla's front door. The co-worker immediately called the Pine Bluff Police Department to report that Darla was missing and possibly hurt.

Deputies from the Pulaski County Sheriff's Office were the first to arrive at the scene, and they were unsure if they were dealing with a simple missing person case or something more sinister. A quick check of the parking lot showed that Darla's car was missing, leading them to wonder if she had driven away from the apartment complex voluntarily. Investigators started going door-to-door in the complex, hoping that some of the other residents might be able to shed some light on the situation.

When investigators spoke with the neighbor who had visited Darla the day before, she told them that Darla had been fine when she left the apartment. Around 11:00 pm, however, the neighbor heard some noises coming from Darla's; it sounded to her as if furniture were being moved. She picked up the phone to call and make sure everything was okay, but the noise had stopped by then. Not wanting to risk waking up Darla's young daughter over something silly, the neighbor hung up the phone without calling. Now, she wished that she had remained on the line.

As soon as Darla's mother learned that she was missing, she knew that something terrible happened. Mel Nixon was adamant that her daughter would never have left Leslie alone under any circumstances. Mel was able to provide detectives with some background information on Darla, including the fact that she and her ex-husband, Barry Harper, had finalized their divorce just four months earlier.

Detectives were eager to speak with Barry, but he denied knowing anything about Darla's disappearance. He was repeatedly questioned by investigators and continued to maintain his innocence. With no evidence linking him to any possible crime, detectives were forced to look elsewhere.

The day after Darla was reported missing, her car was located in a commuter parking lot near Crystal Hill,

Arkansas. This was nine miles away from Darla's apartment, and not in an area where she would normally have driven. There was a small amount of blood found in the car; when the car was brought in for further processing, an unidentified set of fingerprints was also found.

Darla's daughter, Leslie, was just a toddler and detectives knew she wouldn't be considered a competent witness if the case ever went to trial, but they spoke with her anyway. Leslie said things like "Three men came in funny hats" and "Mommy was in a bag, her feet were broken." Due to her young age, it was unclear if she was relating what she had actually seen or if it was fabricated. Either way, it was clear she had witnessed something traumatic.

There were no reported sightings of Darla after she was reported missing, and detectives were convinced that she had been the victim of foul play. They made several appeals to the public for any information that might help them determine what happened to the young mother, but few tips were received.

Six months after Darla went missing, Mel Nixon and her husband, Jerry, announced that they were offering a $10,000 reward for information that led to the recovery of Darla, dead or alive. They were also offering a $16,000 reward for information leading to the arrest and conviction of the person responsible for Darla's death. They hoped that the prospect of a monetary reward would bring in new leads for investigators, but the phones remained silent.

Eventually, detectives exhausted all the leads they were able to develop and the case started to go cold. Although they would periodically review the case file to see if there was anything they might have missed, little progress was made on the case over the next few years.

In 1990, investigators received a tip from Barry Harper's wife at the time; she told them that Darla's remains were buried in the backyard of the home that Barry and Darla had shared prior to the divorce. A search of the property was conducted and some bone fragments were found, but investigators were unable to determine if the bone was human or not.

In 2009, a man was walking his dog in a wooded area of Sherwood, Arkansas when he stumbled upon what he thought was a shallow grave. He immediately phoned police. The only open missing person case in the area was Darla's, and investigators noted that the site was just three miles from Barry Harper's home. A search of the dirt-covered mound was conducted, but nothing of interest was found.

Darla is officially still considered a missing person, but everyone involved in her case is convinced that she is dead. Her daughter was the center of her world, and she was far too close to her family to leave without telling anyone. Over the years, there have been a few sporadic searches for her remains, but nothing has been found to suggest what might have happened to her that March night so many years ago.

As an adult, Leslie noted that she still remembers a few things about the night her mother disappeared, but she was so young when it happened that she isn't sure if she is remembering something that she witnessed or simply recalling things that she was told later. She told one reporter in 2003 that she could remember seeing people wearing all black with ski masks over their faces coming up the stairs. In 1986, she told investigators that her mother's feet were broken; it's likely that she witnessed someone carrying her mother out of the apartment.

Darla's family has been waiting for more than 35 years to learn what happened to her. They have come to terms with the fact that she was most likely killed on the same night she went missing, but they would like to be able to bring her home so they can give her a proper burial. Although the case has been cold for decades, detectives believe that it can still be solved if the right person finally decided to come forward and tell investigators what they know.

Darla Harper was just 25 years old when she went missing from Gravel Ridge, Arkansas in March 1986. She has brown eyes and light brown hair, and at the time of her disappearance, she was 5 feet 4 inches tall and weighed 115 pounds. She was last seen wearing blue jeans and a pullover shirt; she was also wearing a teardrop-shaped diamond pendant, a diamond cluster ring, and a horseshoe-shaped diamond ring. She has a small scar on her right cheek and a burn scar on her left elbow. If you have any information about Darla, please contact the Pulaski County Sheriff's Office at 501-340-6601.

Tomiene Jones

Tomiene Jones dropped her daughter off with a babysitter so she could enjoy a night out with one of her female friends on the evening of April 17, 2002. The 19-year-old postal worker then returned to her apartment in Harrison Township, New Jersey, and waited for her friend to arrive to pick her up for their night out. They had a fun but uneventful evening, and her friend dropped her back off at her apartment around 11:30 pm.

Tomiene – called Meme by her family and friends – called her friend around 1:00 am to make sure she got home safely. The two talked for a few minutes, and her friend would later recall that it sounded like there was someone at Meme's apartment with her, but she wasn't sure who the person was. She didn't give it much thought at the time, and the two friends were off the phone before 1:30 am. Sometime after that, Meme disappeared.

Meme's brother drove to her apartment the following morning after receiving a concerning call from Janiyah's babysitter. She reported that Meme had not returned to pick up her daughter, something that was completely out of character for her. She was a devoted mother who always put her child's needs first, and she had never been late picking her up before. Meme's brother, Tom, immediately had a bad feeling that something was wrong, and he rushed to check on his sister.

When Tom pulled into the parking lot of the Mullica West Apartment complex on Route 45, he could see his sister's 2000 Ford Focus parked in its usual parking spot. He quickly made his way to her apartment, where he was disturbed to find her front door ajar. He cautiously entered the apartment and called out his sister's name, but got no response. When he noticed that her bathroom door had been broken, he realized he was looking at a potential crime scene and slowly backed out of the apartment to call the Harrison Township police.

Meme's car keys and apartment keys were found inside her apartment; her purse, wallet, and identification were located locked inside her car. Except for the broken bathroom door, there was nothing inside the apartment that appeared out of place.

Officers from the Harrison Township Police Department determined very early in their investigation that foul play had likely been involved. Meme was a devoted mother with a steady job and a close relationship with her family, and they knew that she wasn't the kind of person who would voluntarily disappear.

Marc Goodson, the father of Meme's daughter, was a natural person of interest in Meme's disappearance. The two had a rocky relationship that started when Meme was 15 years old. They had broken up and gotten back together on a number of occasions, and she had been forced to take him to court in August 2000 in order to get him to pay child support after Janiyah was born.

Ironically, Marc was arrested the same day that Meme was reported missing, but on completely unrelated charges. The 25-year-old had been involved in a sexual relationship with a 13-year-girl; this was brought to the attention of police after he allegedly videotaped himself during a sexual encounter with the teenager. He had been arrested on sexual assault and molestation charges, and the victim was granted a restraining order against him. He was arrested for violating the restraining order and his bail was revoked. He was interviewed by detectives regarding Meme's disappearance, but he emphatically denied having any involvement in it.

The Harrison Township police were assisted in their search for Meme by the New Jersey State Police and the Gloucester County Prosecutor's Office. They spent two days dredging an area of Alloway Creek in Quinton, New Jersey, and searching the wooded area surrounding it. This was particularly disturbing to Meme's family, as they remembered how Nyoka Brice's body had been found in the creek in April 2000; Nyoka had also dated Marc Goodson at one point and had a child with him. Investigators found nothing related to Meme's disappearance, however, and the family breathed a slight sigh of relief. They wanted to find Meme, but they wanted to find her alive.

Meme's family had never been happy about her relationship with Marc; there were allegations of abuse and they didn't feel that he treated her right. At one point, Meme had gone into hiding at a women's shelter and made it clear that she didn't want Marc to know where she was living. They would always make up, however, and she continued to see him. Meme's sister-in-law described her as being a very sweet girl, but not very street-smart. She was easily swayed by Marc.

The main reason she had decided to move into her own apartment the previous year was so she could spend time with Marc without having to deal with her family's disapproval of him, but even after she moved out she remained in close contact with her parents and brother.

Investigators spoke to a couple of people who were friends with both Marc and Meme, and they told detectives that the couple appeared to have a strong relationship. They claimed they had never seen the pair fight, but detectives had police reports that contradicted this claim.

About a month before she went missing, Meme had filed assault charges against Marc, claiming that he had punched her in her chest, causing her to fall backward into her bathtub. When she fell, she injured her back. He had been arrested but was able to bail himself out of jail. Marc and Meme were not supposed to have any contact after that, but a few weeks later Meme was arrested and charged with simple assault, harassment, and contempt of court after she and Marc got into an altercation. Meme was not particularly worried about the charges; she was confident when she went to court that the judge would understand she had been acting in her own self-defense when she struck Marc with an umbrella.

Although some believed that Marc had been involved in both the murder of Nyoka and the disappearance of Meme, there was no tangible evidence against him in either case. Even Meme's parents were unsure about Marc's involvement in Nyoka's murder; they noted that Nyoka had many enemies and there were a number of people who might have wanted her dead. Police were unsure about Marc's involvement as well, and no suspects were ever named in the unsolved murder case.

Meme, however, did not have any known enemies. She had a good job with the postal service and she spent most of her time away from work with her daughter. Marc continued to deny that he had anything to do with her disappearance; he claimed he had not spoken to her since the day before she went missing. Detectives searched his home on April 25; although they found cocaine and other evidence of drug use, they found nothing to support the theory that Marc had harmed Meme.

71

Investigators knew they couldn't afford to get tunnel vision, and they continued to follow up on all tips they received. Unfortunately, they were unable to develop solid leads, and Meme's whereabouts remained unknown. They spent days going through creeks, streams, and other waterways in Salem County, New Jersey. They scoured the Salem River and some of its estuaries, then moved on to Mannington Lake. They used motorbikes and a helicopter to search the areas surrounding the lake, taking special care to go through all the areas where they knew a body might wash up with the tide. They found absolutely nothing.

Meme's father, Thomas, had always had a close relationship with the daughter he named after himself. He was devastated by her disappearance and spent days combing through various wooded areas in Salem County, praying for some sort of clue that would lead to Meme. Like investigators, his search came up empty.

Six weeks into the investigation, authorities announced that they believed that Meme had most likely been murdered, and confirmed that they had a suspect in her death; although they did not mention any names, it was clear they were talking about Marc.

The investigation seemed to stall soon after this, as detectives were unable to locate Meme or any evidence against Marc. In November, they announced that they were offering a $9,000 reward for information leading to the arrest and conviction of the person responsible for Meme's disappearance.

Marc wrote to Meme's family while he was in prison, and assured them that he had loved Meme and had nothing to do with her disappearance. In January 2003, he was interviewed by a reporter, and he readily admitted to committing several crimes, including assault,

72

sex with a minor, and dealing drugs. He continued to maintain that he was not involved in Meme's disappearance. Police interrogated him numerous times and searched his home, but they were unable to find any evidence against him.

Over the years, Meme's family has continued to search tirelessly for her, and have praised the Gloucester County Prosecutor's Office for the way they kept the investigation active. In August 2003, the family raised money to have two billboards placed along area highways to make sure the public didn't forget that Meme was still missing. Although the billboards brought in a few tips, no substantial leads resulted.

Thomas and Cheryl Jones took over the responsibility for raising Janiyah, who eventually realized that her mother was not going to come home. Although they tried to make sure she got to experience a normal childhood, holiday celebrations were always tinged with sadness because Meme was missing. Not having a gravesite to visit and leave flowers was one of the hardest things for the family; they just wanted to be able to bring Meme home.

Meme's parents made several public pleas for information but admitted that they believed Marc was the one person who could tell them where to find Meme. He continued to maintain his innocence, and he was never publicly named a suspect.

By the time she was in high school, Janiyah had grown into a young woman who looked a lot like her mother. Meme had once dreamed of going to school to become a veterinarian, and now Janiyah had the same goal.

Thomas and Cheryl continue to hold out hope that they will one day learn what happened to their daughter.

They cling to a sliver of hope that she might be alive somewhere, though rationally they know this is not the case. Still, even after more than two decades, they have not declared Meme legally dead; that would make everything seem far too real.

Tomiene Mary Jones was just 19 years old when she went missing from Harrison Township, New Jersey in April 2002. She has brown eyes and black hair, and at the time of her disappearance, she was 5 feet 5 inches tall and weighed 135 pounds. She was last seen wearing an orange, red, and white dress. If you have any information about Tomiene, please contact the Gloucester County Prosecutor's Office at 856-384-5602 or the Harrison Township Police Department at 856-468-8600.

Bethany Markowski

Bethany Markowski was a typical 11-year-old girl who loved to shop. She asked her father, Larry Markowski, if they could stop at a nearby shopping mall so she could go to an accessories shop there, and he reluctantly agreed. He pulled into the parking lot of the Old Hickory Mall in Jackson, Tennessee around 2:30 pm on Sunday, March 4, 2001. He told Bethany that he would wait for her in the parking lot; he was still exhausted from the weekend and figured he could doze off for a bit while she was shopping. He reminded his daughter not to take too long, as they had to meet her aunt later that afternoon. Bethany promised to come back as soon as she was finished shopping and hopped out of the truck. He watched as she headed towards the entrance of the mall, then closed his eyes and fell asleep.

Larry and Jonnie Markowski were in the process of getting a divorce, and their daughter Bethany was caught in the middle. Jonnie and Bethany had moved out of the family home in Gleason, Tennessee, and were staying with Jonnie's sister in Nashville. Although Jonnie retained primary custody of Bethany, the court had granted Larry visitation rights and he was entitled to see his daughter every other weekend.

The couple's split had been so contentious that Jonnie had taken out a restraining order against Larry, so her sister, Lori, had agreed to drive Bethany back and forth from her weekend visitations. She and Larry would meet in Waverly, Tennessee, halfway between Gleason and

Nashville, for the custody exchange. Lori had dropped Bethany off there on Friday, and Larry promised to have her back by 5:00 pm on Sunday. Since Waverly was about an hour and a half from the Old Hickory Mall, Bethany had about an hour to shop before they would need to be back on the road.

According to Larry, he dozed off for about a half hour, and when he saw that Bethany hadn't returned he decided to go into the mall and look for her. She had said she wanted to go to Claire's Boutique and possibly the video arcade, so he checked these places first. When he was unable to find her, he started searching through the rest of the mall, but she wasn't in any of the shops. After checking the truck to make sure she hadn't slipped past him, he reported her missing to mall security and they phoned the Jackson Police Department.

Larry's first weekend visitation with Bethany had taken place two weeks before, and it had been uneventful. He had returned with Bethany at the appointed time, and Lori expected this weekend would be the same. She realized something was wrong when she hadn't seen any sign of Larry or Bethany by 6:00 pm. Unsure what to do, she tried to call Larry's home but received no answer. Eventually, Jonnie was contacted by the Jackson police who let her know that Bethany was missing. It was the beginning of a nightmare for Jonnie, and she immediately drove to Jackson, Tennessee to join in the search for her daughter.

Larry and Jonnie's relationship had likely been doomed from the start. When they first started dating, he told Jonnie that he was separated from his wife, who had taken the kids and moved to Alabama. It wasn't until Jonnie was already pregnant with Bethany that she learned Larry was actually still married and was living with his wife and children. He did end up getting a divorce, though, and soon married Jonnie. He was thrilled when Bethany was born, and was a great father to her. Jonnie claimed that he got more controlling as Bethany grew older, and there were allegations of domestic violence in the home. Eventually, Jonnie had enough. She filed for divorce and moved with Bethany to Nashville.

Jonnie initially tried to keep their location secret from Larry, but he learned where she was staying and showed up at Bethany's school one day. According to Jonnie, he tried to take Bethany from the school but several teachers intervened. It was at this point that Jonnie obtained a restraining order against her ex-husband, but she couldn't prevent him from seeing Bethany as he was awarded visitation rights.

According to Larry, after he picked Bethany up on Friday, they had spent time with friends in Little Rock, Arkansas before returning to Gleason on Sunday morning. Larry stated that he had been up most of the night driving back to Tennessee, and that was why he wanted to take a nap while Bethany went shopping. He admitted that, in hindsight, he shouldn't have allowed her to go into the mall alone, but Bethany had grown up in the area and was very familiar with the Old Hickory Mall. He believed it was safe to let her go inside without him since she had been in the mall so many times before.

Bethany was a sweet and funny child who could also have an attitude when things weren't going her way. It's possible that she did convince her father to stop at the mall because she wanted to go shopping, but police could find no evidence of this on mall security cameras. Despite viewing all the footage taken on the day Bethany disappeared, they were unable to confirm that she ever made it into the mall.

Detectives interviewed Larry extensively, but he continued to maintain that he had last seen Bethany as she was walking across the parking lot toward the mall. He did not see her actually enter the mall, but assumed she made it inside. Investigators were skeptical and initially believed that Larry might have hidden Bethany somewhere in an attempt to gain full custody of her, albeit by illegal means. Despite an intense investigation, however, they were unable to find any evidence to support this theory.

Detectives believed that Bethany might have been abducted by someone as she made her way across the mall parking lot, but Jonnie was certain that Bethany would have created a scene if anyone had tried to force her into a car. She had taught Bethany to kick and scream if she ever found herself confronted by a stranger. If she had been taken by someone, they must have found some way to gain her trust first. There were no security cameras in the parking lot of the mall, and no one reported seeing anything unusual.

Police searched the entire mall and the surrounding area for hours Sunday night, but found no clues as to what had happened to Bethany. Realizing that the situation was not going to be resolved quickly, Jonnie and Lori returned to Nashville on Monday morning to pack some clothes and print up some missing person flyers. On their way back to Jackson, they stopped at every truck stop and gas station they passed to hang up Bethany's missing poster.

Despite numerous searches, days turned into weeks without any progress being made on the case. Detectives were unable to find any witnesses who had seen Bethany on the day she disappeared, and there were no reported sightings of her in the following weeks. Then, about a month after Bethany went missing, police were alerted that a woman had tried to enroll a girl who looked like Bethany in a school in eastern Tennessee. She was described as a blonde white woman in her 40s, and she had left without enrolling the child because she didn't have the proper paperwork for her.

In late April 2001, employees at a restaurant in Cleveland, Tennessee reported seeing a girl matching Bethany's description on three consecutive days. Each time she was with the same blonde woman. The pair allegedly boarded a bus going to Moline, Illinois; police checked the bus when it reached its destination but were unable to locate the woman or the child. Although these sightings couldn't be confirmed, Bethany's mother believes that the child was her daughter and that the woman was likely one of Larry's relatives. Detectives pursued this lead for months but were never able to make any connection to Bethany or Larry's family.

Detectives continue to actively investigate Bethany's case, and they still believe that the case is solvable. They are aware of the fact that parental abductions are far more common than stranger abductions, and over the years they have considered both possibilities. According to the Tennessee Bureau of Investigations, there is no information to suggest that Jonnie was involved in her daughter's disappearance, and though they have never been able to conclusively rule Larry out as a suspect, they have no evidence to show that he was involved. They also have been unable to rule out the possibility that Bethany was abducted by a stranger.

Bethany Markowski was just 11 years old when she went missing from Jackson, Tennessee in March 2001. She has brown hair and green eyes, and at the time of her disappearance, she was 4 feet 10 inches tall and weighed approximately 100 pounds. She was last seen wearing a green t-shirt, black or blue jeans, and black slip-on shoes. She was missing her top and bottom baby molars at the time, and she had freckles on her cheeks and nose. She also had a habit of biting her fingernails when she was nervous. If you have any information about Bethany, please contact the Jackson Police Department at 731-425-8400 or the Tennessee Bureau of Investigation at 1-800-824-3463.

Nita Mayo

Nita Mayo had the day off from work and decided to go on a road trip on August 8, 2005. The 64-year-old had breakfast with a friend in her hometown of Hawthorne, Nevada, then set off alone around 11:00 am. She wanted to drive to Sonora, California, located 175 miles to the west of Hawthorne. Her planned route would take her over Sonora Pass, one of the highest mountain roads in the state of California. Known for its spectacular scenery, the high mountain pass was only open for about half the year, closing once winter weather rolled in and reopening around May 15th. Nita brought her camera so she could take some pictures of the trip, and she also planned to do some shopping at some of the souvenir stores that lined her chosen route. She told friends she would return home later that evening, in plenty of time to report for her nursing shift the following morning.

Nita, who had been born in England, had always been the perfect mix of cautious and adventurous. She had married an American who was serving in the Air Force and moved to the United States with him. They had four children who were born and raised in Oklahoma, and they had many fond memories of taking impromptu road trips with their mother. Once they had grown up and had families of their own, Nita decided to move from Oklahoma to Nevada. A licensed practical nurse, she had lined up a job at Mt. Grant General Hospital in Hawthorne and moved herself across the country 15 years earlier. She loved exploring the diverse scenery the West had to offer, and would often take day trips by herself.

Nita got into her 1997 silver Mercury Sable station wagon and began the trip west. The weather was perfect and it appeared to be a great day for sightseeing; Nita was just one of many tourists who traveled along Sonora Pass that Monday.

Nita lived alone, so there was no one waiting for her at home to notice that she never made it back to Nevada. Her co-workers at Mt. Grant General Hospital sounded the alarm when she failed to show up for her scheduled shift on Tuesday morning; Nita had always been a reliable and dependable employee who never missed work. Repeated calls to her home went unanswered, and her co-workers were particularly concerned because they knew she had planned to take a day trip to California. A co-worker drove to Nita's home and immediately noticed that her car wasn't there. Afraid she might have been in some kind of accident, they called the Mineral County Sheriff's Office and reported her missing.

When deputies from the Mineral County Sheriff's Office learned about the missing woman's road trip, they alerted law enforcement agencies along the route to Sonora. They also had to phone Nita's four children and tell them that their mother was missing. Her children, who lived in three different states, assumed that their mother had likely had some kind of accident resulting in her car running off the road, and they made plans to head west.

On Wednesday, a deputy from the Tuolumne County Sheriff's Department located Nita's car in the parking lot at Donnell Vista, a scenic outlook located along Sonora Pass. The car was locked, and there was no sign of Nita anywhere. Authorities immediately conducted a search of the surrounding area but found no clues as to Nita's whereabouts. A Caltrans worker reported to police that they had seen the car parked in the lot on Monday evening as well as Tuesday morning, but since the parking lot was often used by backpackers who would stay overnight in the forest, the car didn't arouse any suspicions.

The news that Nita's car had been found abandoned stunned her children. They had hoped that once Nita's car was located, she would be with it. Tracy, who lived in North Dakota, was the first of the siblings to arrive in California. She was frantic with worry and desperate to find her mother. She was soon joined by her brother, Pete, who lived in Tennessee, and her sisters, Shelly and Cindy, who lived in Oklahoma.

Although search and rescue teams were in the process of searching the area surrounding where Nita's car was found, her children conducted their own search. They first drove to Donnell Vista and parked in the same lot their mother had parked in days earlier. From the parking lot, there was a one-quarter-mile paved trail that led to an overlook with views of Donnell Reservoir and the Middle Fork Stanislaus River Canyon. They were shocked by the rugged and unforgiving terrain of the Stanislaus Forest, and they knew that their mother would not have strayed from the paved trail.

Nita's car had been locked when it was found, and it appeared that she had left most of her belongings, including her car keys, inside it. This was Nita's normal habit, as the car had an electronic keypad that could be used to unlock the doors, and she preferred to use that. Her purse, wallet, identification, credit cards, money, and cell phone were found locked inside, as well as a sweatshirt, a water bottle, and a canvas folding chair in a canvas bag.

Also found in the car were some souvenirs that had

been purchased from the Strawberry General Store in Strawberry, California, about 15 miles west of Donnell Vista. A receipt found in the car showed that Nita had bought some postcards and a refrigerator magnet at the store around 4:30 pm. At some point after that, she had started to make the journey back to Nevada, apparently stopping at Donnell Vista on her way home.

The only items that appeared to be missing from the car were Nita's camera and her prescription sunglasses. This supported the theory that she had gotten out of the car expecting to take some pictures of the area.

A search dog was brought to the scene in the hopes he could track the direction Nita might have gone after she parked her car, but the dog was only able to follow her scent a few feet from the car.

Detectives could see no overt signs of foul play near the car but had it towed for forensic processing. It would take some time to get the results, but they eventually determined that all the fingerprints found inside the car belonged to Nita, and there was nothing to indicate any kind of foul play had taken place inside the car.

Authorities initially believed that Nita must have wandered off the trail and gotten lost in the forest, and they spent days combing through the area looking for any clues that might lead them to Nita. Search and rescue teams with extensive experience working in rugged terrain like that of Stanislaus Forest found nothing to indicate that anyone had fallen off the trail, as there were no drag marks, torn clothing, broken branches, or trampled vegetation.

Search teams from Calaveras, Mono, and Tuolumne Counties all participated in the search for Nita, and they spent the rest of the week combing through the area around Donnell Vista. A number of canine units were used, but they failed to find any sign of the missing woman. A helicopter team from the California Highway Patrol made numerous passes over the steep, rocky canyons scanning for anything that appeared out of place, but were unable to find anything.

By Saturday, it was clear that authorities were beginning to think that they were not going to find Nita alive, but her children refused to give up hope. They continued their own search throughout the weekend; aided by local volunteers, they spent hours hiking through the canyons, scouring various campgrounds, and driving up and down old logging roads. They were consumed by the thought that their mother might be lost and hurt and in desperate need of help. Unfortunately, like authorities, they failed to find anything that led them closer to Nita.

Some people feared that Nita might have wandered too close to the edge of a cliff while taking pictures, then lost her footing and fell. Her children doubted that their mother would have gone off the trail, though, and couldn't imagine that she would go anywhere near any of the cliffs in the area. She was always very cautious about safety, and the kind of hiker who always stuck to marked trails.

Experts from Yosemite Mountaineering were called in to assist with the search, and they rappelled down from the overlook, a 750-foot drop. They found nothing to indicate that anyone had fallen over the side, and no clues were located on the ground below, either. There was no trace of Nita, her camera, or her sunglasses.

Over the next week, extensive searches of the Donnell Vista area continued to be conducted. A group of Marines from the Mountain Warfare Training Center in Mono County volunteered to help the search and rescue teams. Dogs and helicopters were also used, and all trails and campgrounds along the Stanislaus River canyon were searched. By the time the week was over, authorities concluded that Nita was not on the mountain or at the bottom of it. They still had absolutely no idea where she might be.

Nita's children spent the week hanging up missing person posters all over the area. They also canvassed neighborhoods and businesses located near Donnell Vista, distributing missing person flyers and talking with people to see if anyone recalled seeing anything unusual the day that Nita disappeared. They went up and down Highway 108, making sure each rest area and gas station had their mother's missing poster displayed.

Ten days into their search, Nita's family remained optimistic that they would find their mother alive, but they were afraid that she had been abducted and taken out of the area. They continued scouring the area around Donnell Vista, but repeated searches had failed to turn up anything related to Nita.

The Carole Sund-Carrington Memorial Reward Foundation reached out to Nita's family and offered a $5,000 reward for information leading to the safe return of Nita. If she had been the victim of foul play, the money would be paid out to anyone with information leading to the arrest and conviction of the person responsible.

With the help of volunteers, missing person flyers were distributed all across California and Nevada, and word began to spread about the missing woman. That weekend, a man in Reno called police to report seeing a woman matching Nita's description in a local shopping market. He said that the woman appeared disheveled and disoriented. Believing that the man might have actually seen Nita, her son raced to Reno to view surveillance footage from the market to see if he could recognize her. Unfortunately, he was unable to confirm that the man had seen his mother.

Nita's family made the decision to remain in California for the foreseeable future; it meant putting their lives on hold, but they were desperate to locate their mother. When they learned this, Nita's co-workers at the hospital raised $1200 and donated to the family to help them with some of their expenses. Several of her co-workers also made the drive to California and assisted in the physical search for the missing nurse.

Although authorities stopped conducting large-scale searches for Nita, investigators continued to follow up on all leads they received. The case was particularly puzzling because they had so little information; there was nothing to indicate that foul play had taken place, no evidence that Nita had fallen or gotten lost and never made it back to her car, and absolutely nothing to suggest that Nita would simply walk away from her life.

During their investigation, detectives learned that a woman from Colorado Springs had been seen in Strawberry around the same time Nita had been there, and the woman had been asking people for help because her vehicle had broken down. They released the name and the description of the woman in an attempt to locate her, believing she might have witnessed something that was pertinent to their investigation. Although they didn't say so directly, they seemed to infer that it was possible Nita might have offered the woman a ride. It took several months to find the woman, and when they did she was unable to provide them with any helpful information. It didn't appear that she and Nita had ever crossed paths.

Knowing that Donnell Vista was a major tourist attraction, Nita's family realized that it was possible that someone who lived out of the area might have been visiting the overlook on the day that Nita disappeared, and they might have seen something without realizing that it could be important to a missing person investigation. With that in mind, they tried to get national publicity for the case, hoping to reach potential witnesses. Although they managed to line up a few interviews on a couple of cable news programs, each time they were scheduled to speak about Nita, their interviews were canceled at the last minute. Hurricane Katrina and the disappearance of Natalee Holloway were deemed to be more nationally relevant news stories.

Nita's children remained in California for more than a month, but eventually, they had to reluctantly return home so they could go back to work and take care of their families. They returned to the area frequently, however, refusing to allow local residents and law enforcement to forget their mother was missing.

They held various fundraisers to aid them in their continued search, and they found that both the California and Nevada communities were extremely generous with their time and money. Yet by the time the first snowfall arrived and Sonora Pass was closed for the winter, they still had no idea what might have happened to their beloved mother. It was a devastating blow, and they were forced to confront the fact that their mother was likely not going to be found alive.

The family continued to return to the area each year around the anniversary of Nita's disappearance, organizing searches and making sure that her missing poster was still being prominently displayed along Highway 108. They also took time to recognize those in the community who had helped them in the search for Nita.

Nita was declared legally dead in 2013, but her

family continues to search for her remains. Over the years, they have had a bench dedicated to Nita placed at the Donnell Vista, and a plaque installed at the Strawberry General Store where she made her final purchases. A copy of her missing poster still hangs outside the emergency room door of Mt. Grant General Hospital.

The Tuolumne County Sheriff's Department states that Nita's case remains active, and it has not been turned over to the cold case division as of 2023. Detectives believe they still have legitimate leads to follow and hope to one day be able to resolve the case.

Nita Mary Mayo was 64 years old when she went missing from Sonora, California in August 2005. She has hazel eyes and brown hair, and at the time of the disappearance, she was 5 feet 1 inch tall and weighed about 140 pounds. It is not known what clothing she was wearing at the time of her disappearance, but she usually preferred capri pants and light cotton shirts, and she was carrying a camera and prescription sunglasses. She was wearing several pieces of jewelry when she went missing, including a gold mother's ring with four colored gemstones, one each of green, pink, blue, and purple; a Celtic style silver necklace, and a silver necklace with a pendant that had one blue stone and two pink stones. Nita was born in England and spoke with an English accent. If you have any information about Nita, please contact the Tuolumne County Sheriff's Department at 209-533-5815 or Secret Witness at 775-322-4900. A reward is being offered for information that leads to the recovery of Nita or the arrest and conviction of the person responsible for her disappearance.

Jennifer Pandos

Jennifer Pandos was extremely upset on February 9, 1987. The 15-year-old told some of her friends that she and her boyfriend had been fighting, and she was very distraught about it. She spent the evening at her home in Williamsburg, Virginia, where she lived with her mother and father; they didn't notice anything unusual about her behavior and she didn't mention anything about having problems with her boyfriend.

Jenny was a sophomore at Lafayette High School in James City County, Virginia, just outside her hometown of Williamsburg. She was a friendly and popular student who enjoyed the social aspects of high school, and she rarely missed class.

On the morning of February 10, 1987, Margie Pandos was surprised when 6:00 am came and went and she didn't hear the sounds of her daughter getting into the shower. Jenny was extremely predictable in the morning and was always in the shower by 6:00 am so she would have enough time to get dressed and do her hair before leaving for school.

Assuming that Jenny had overslept, Margie knocked on her bedroom door. When she didn't get a reply, she tried to enter Jenny's bedroom but found the door locked. This was also surprising; Jenny always slept with her door unlocked. Margie woke up her husband, Ron, and the two of them were able to force their way into Jenny's bedroom.

They weren't sure what they would find when they

opened the door, but they were met with only silence. Jenny wasn't in her room. The first thing they noticed was that one of the window blinds had been bent down, as if Jenny had been trying to look out the window from between the blinds.

As Margie and Ron scanned around the room, trying desperately to determine what was going on, they saw that Jenny had left a note on her pillow. It didn't appear to be written in Jenny's handwriting, and it started with "Your daughter's with me. She's fine. She's having some problems and needs some time away."

The second paragraph of the note was written in the same handwriting as the first, but sounded as if it had been written by Jenny: "I'm fine. I just need time to think." The note then instructed Margie and Ron to go to work as usual if they wanted to hear from Jenny. "Both of you please go to work tomorrow 'cause I will try to call you. I won't call you at home, only at one of y'all's work."

As if anticipating their next move, the note then instructed Jenny's parents to leave the police out of it. "Do not call the police. I can easily find out if you do. I may never come back home. Don't tell my friends about this. Just tell them that I'm sick."

Margie and Ron weren't sure what to do. They wanted to call the police, but they were afraid that doing so might mean they would never see their daughter again. As they looked around Jenny's room, they realized that the only thing the teenager had taken with her had been her purse. She hadn't even taken a coat with her, despite the freezing February temperatures.

All of Jenny's clothing, shoes, makeup, and other belongings were still in her room. They took this as a hopeful sign that she would indeed be back soon. They couldn't imagine that Jenny would go anywhere for an extended period of time without being able to change her clothes and do her makeup. Reluctantly, they decided to go to work as usual and hope that Jenny called one of them to let them know exactly what was going on with her.

The day passed without any contact from Jenny. Margie had spent most of her time at work staring at the phone, willing it to ring. She wasn't sure what to think when Jenny didn't call. She wanted to call the police, but she and Ron decided to wait for a couple of days. Perhaps Jenny would call one of them the following day.

After three days without any contact from the teenager, Margie called the Williamsburg Police Department and reported Jenny missing. She showed detectives the note that Jenny had left and told them that even though it didn't look like Jenny's handwriting, the wording did sound like her daughter and she thought it was possible that she had indeed written it. Some of the investigators who examined the note speculated that Jenny, who was left-handed, had written the note with her right hand in order to disguise her handwriting.

Detectives were extremely interested in speaking with Jenny's boyfriend, Tony Tobler, and they brought him in for questioning. He admitted that the couple had been having some problems, and their relationship had always been an on-and-off one. He was adamant that he had nothing to do with Jenny's disappearance; like all of her friends, he was surprised to learn that she was missing in the first place. Everyone had assumed that she had not been in school because she was sick.

After interviewing him several times, detectives eventually determined that Tony was telling the truth and was not involved in Jenny's disappearance. At this point, they weren't even sure that a crime had occurred. The teen had left a note saying that she was leaving because she needed time to think about some things; to investigators, it was apparent that she had run away voluntarily. There was little police would do in this case.

The James City County Police Department was assigned Jenny's case, and about a month after she went missing they made a public plea for help in determining her location. They also announced that they were offering a $500 reward for any information that led to her whereabouts. They received few calls, and though they did follow up on all tips that came in, none of them led to the missing teenager.

Although Jenny was initially considered to be a runaway, as months went by without any contact from her – and no reported sightings of her – investigators began to fear that she might have run into foul play. Even if she had left her parents' home willingly, the streets were no place for a 15-year-old girl, and it was very possible that something had happened to her after she left the safety of her home.

Detectives were unable to come up with any reason why Jenny would have wanted to run away from home in the first place. She had no problems with her mother or father, she was doing well in school, and she didn't use alcohol or drugs. She hadn't been fighting with any of her friends, and except for her on-again-off-again relationship with Tony, she seemed to have no reason to leave her comfortable life behind.

The note that she left was also somewhat questionable. Although everyone involved believed that Jenny had written the note, why had she felt the need to disguise her handwriting? It's possible that she was trying, indirectly, to let someone know that she was being forced to write the note by some unknown person.

Although investigators spoke with Jenny's family, boyfriend, friends, and classmates, none of them were able to offer any insight into where Jenny might have gone. Many of them felt that Jenny wouldn't have run off without saying something to at least one of her friends, but none of them ever heard from her.

Despite the monetary reward that was offered for information about Jenny's whereabouts, the case quickly stalled and went cold. It remains that way today. Detectives still aren't sure if Jenny is alive or dead, though after more than 30 years with no contact, they assume the worst. They have conducted several searches of the Williamsburg area using cadaver dogs, but they have never found any evidence related to Jenny's case.

Jenny's older brother, Steven, was away at college when she vanished and later told people that he always suspected his parents had something to do with her disappearance. They denied the claims and detectives recently indicated that they believe Jenny's boyfriend might have been involved. As of August 2023, no one has been charged in connection with Jenny's disappearance and the case remains open.

Jennifer Lynn Pandos was just 15 years old when she went missing from Williamsburg, Virginia in February 1987. She has hazel eyes and brown hair, and at the time of her disappearance she was 5 feet 2 inches tall and weighed 100 pounds. She was last seen wearing blue jeans, a nightshirt with a picture of a panda on the front, a pink sweater, a pink nylon waist-length jacket, and white high-top sneakers. She is left-handed and has a small mole on her left shoulder. If you have any information about Jenny, please contact the James City County Police Department at 757-253-1800.

Bianca Piper

Bianca Piper could be a handful. The 13-year-old had problems with anger management and was being treated for several mental disorders, including ADHD and bipolar disorder. She had the mental capacity of a second grader. Although she was on several prescription medications to control her symptoms, there were times when she couldn't control her anger and would lash out at people. March 10, 2005 was one of those days. Bianca didn't want to do the dishes after dinner, and a small argument escalated until she had a complete meltdown. A therapist had suggested the best thing to do in these situations was to have Bianca take a long walk to calm down; this technique had worked the night before, so Bianca's mother, Shannon Tanner, decided to try it again.

The previous night, Shannon had dropped her daughter a half mile from their home in Foley, Missouri. When Bianca returned home, she was in a much better mood and told her mother that the walk had been quite easy. On this night, Shannon thought Bianca would benefit from a longer walk, so she doubled the distance, dropping her off about a mile from their home. It was starting to get dark, so she gave Bianca a flashlight, then turned the car around and watched as Bianca started walking toward their house. As Shannon drove past her, she reminded her not to get in a car with anyone and to come straight home.

After sitting at home for nearly an hour with no sign of Bianca, Shannon started to get worried. She got back in her car and started driving toward the spot where she had let Bianca out. She fully expected to find the teenager meandering down the street, but the road was empty. Shannon and her boyfriend then started to go door-to-door in the area, asking if anyone had seen Bianca. No one had. Panicked, Shannon returned home and called police. Responding officers thought it was likely that Bianca had simply decided not to go straight home, but they became increasingly concerned as the night wore on and the temperature dropped well below freezing. Bianca was wearing only jeans and a hooded sweatshirt, and they knew she wouldn't be able to survive long in the frigid cold.

Shannon took police to the area where she had last seen her daughter. They were unable to find any clues about what might have happened to her. There was nothing to indicate any kind of roadside struggle had taken place and no signs of a hit-and-run accident. The road was not heavily trafficked – Shannon recalled seeing only one other car when she had driven along it earlier – and they found no witnesses who had seen the teenager walking that night.

By the next morning, there was still no sign of the missing teenager and police launched an extensive search of the area. More than 100 officers, on foot, on horseback, or in helicopters, took part in the search. A series of checkpoints were set up along the streets of Foley, and all motorists who drove through the area were stopped and questioned. Volunteer firefighters went door-to-door, speaking with residents and getting permission to search their sheds and other structures in case Bianca had sought shelter there. Police combed through the rugged terrain surrounding Bianca's neighborhood. They found nothing.

Shannon and her live-in boyfriend, Jim Pelt, were both interviewed by police numerous times. Shannon, as the last person to see Bianca, faced the most intense scrutiny. There were many people in the community who questioned her decision to let Bianca walk home alone in the dark, but Shannon was adamant that she only did so because it had been recommended to her by Bianca's therapist and admitted she wished she hadn't done so. Eventually, both Shannon and Jim passed polygraph examinations and were eliminated as suspects.

That Tuesday, Shannon and Bianca's father, David Piper, held a press conference to let the public know Bianca was still missing. They explained that she had been in therapy since she was four years old and took medication to control her mood swings and aggressive tendencies. Though she looked like a normal teenage girl – at 5 feet 6 inches and 185 pounds no one would mistake her for a child – she was in desperate need of these medications. She normally took them twice a day; without them, it was likely she would become confused and possibly hallucinate.

Over the next couple of days, more than 200 people helped search for Bianca, covering nearly 150 miles of difficult terrain. They scoured caves and trudged through swamps, all to no avail. They found nothing to suggest that Bianca was still in the area. Police did uncover two different methamphetamine labs, but found nothing to suggest they had anything to do with Bianca's disappearance. Although police said they found nothing to indicate a kidnapping had taken place, Shannon believed that her daughter might have been naïve enough to get into a car with someone who then harmed her.

As days went by without any reported sightings of Bianca, investigators began to fear the worst. They were certain that she wasn't simply lost in the woods; if she had been, they would have already found her. Hoping to drum up some new leads, a reward was offered. They followed up on each of the 130 tips they received, but all led to dead ends.

Three months after Bianca went missing, the case was back in the headlines after Shannon Tanner was arrested for domestic assault on her 17-year-old daughter. The teenager called police after Shannon hit her in the head with a curling iron, repeatedly punched her in the face, and threatened to tie her up and lock her in a bedroom. When officers got to the home, Shannon was on top of her daughter and had to be physically removed by police. When told she was under arrest, Shannon shoved a deputy and began reaching for a piece of broken glass. One of the officers tased her. Subdued, she was arrested and released after posting bond. Although police told the media Shannon had already been cleared as a suspect in Bianca's disappearance, her arrest had a detrimental effect on how the community looked at her and brought increased scrutiny to her parenting skills.

By September, Bianca had been missing for six months and the case was starting to grow cold. Her disappearance had been featured on a national television show, and thousands of postcards with her information were mailed out across the country, but there had been no confirmed sightings of Bianca. Out of desperation, Shannon had even consulted several psychics but got no useful information from them.

A year into the investigation, police noted they had followed up on 338 leads from as far away as Oregon. They had investigated numerous potential sightings of Bianca, but none of them turned out to be the missing teenager. Some detectives believed that Bianca had met foul play at the hands of a local, and was possibly still being held somewhere. The road she went missing from was rarely used by anyone from outside the town of Foley; the chance of a stranger passing by at the exact time Bianca was walking seemed exceedingly remote. Although they would continue to conduct sporadic searches, Bianca's case eventually ended up in the cold case file, where it remains today.

Bianca Noel Piper was just 13 years old when she went missing from Foley, Missouri in March 2005. Bianca suffers from ADHD and bipolar disorder; she has trouble with self-control and can be aggressive with people. She has brown eyes and brown hair, and at the time of her disappearance, she was 5 feet 6 inches tall and weighed 185 pounds. Bianca has scars on her abdomen, arms, and legs. She was last seen wearing blue jeans, a green shirt, a gray hooded sweatshirt, and white sneakers; she was carrying a flashlight. If you have any information about Bianca, please contact the Lincoln County Sheriff's Office at 636-528-8546.

Felipe Santos & Terrance Williams

At first glance, Felipe Santos and Terrance Williams seem to have little in common other than the fact that each had moved to Florida in the hopes of building a better life for themselves. Though they lived in the same county, there is nothing to suggest that their paths ever crossed. It wasn't until they disappeared just three months apart from each other that their names would become permanently linked.

Felipe, a Mexican citizen, was the second of five brothers and had spent much of his life in the rural state of Oaxaca. He had a reputation for being humble and hardworking, but jobs were scarce in his impoverished hometown. Tired of living in poverty, Felipe, his wife Apolonia, and two of his brothers, Jorge and Salvador, entered the United States illegally in 2000. Their main reason for coming to America was to obtain employment, and their job search eventually took them to Florida. They ended up in Immokalee, an area of Collier County that was saturated with farmland. The majority of the workforce here was made up of Mexican, Haitian, and Guatemalan immigrants. Many would only remain in the United States for a short time, preferring to save most of their earnings and then return to their home countries. The Santos family fit right in.

Felipe had experience as a concrete worker, and he had hoped to find a job in the construction industry.

Unfortunately, the transient nature of the population around Immokalee meant there was little need for the newly constructed housing developments that were popping up throughout much of Florida, and construction jobs were essentially non-existent. There was a perpetual need for migrant farmers, though, and all three brothers quickly found work in that area. While they still hoped to eventually find construction work, farming provided them with an immediate source of income. They spent little on themselves; most of what they earned was sent to relatives in their hometown of Oaxaca.

Towards the end of 2002, Felipe and his wife learned that she was pregnant with their first child. By this point, they had been living in the United States for almost three years, and the Santos brothers had earned a reputation for being hard-working and reliable. Much of their time was spent at work, and what little free time they had was usually spent at home. Knowing he would soon have a child to support, Felipe found a job doing construction work in a neighboring county. He would be making more money, but the bigger paycheck came at a price. While the brothers had been able to walk to their farming jobs, the construction site was 30 miles away from their home. Neither walking nor public transportation was a viable option, so Felipe decided to get a car. It was a decision that would have heartbreaking consequences.

Felipe was a competent driver but his status as an illegal alien made it impossible for him to obtain a Florida driver's license. Without a valid license, he was unable to comply with other state laws pertaining to driving – he couldn't register his car or purchase car insurance. He knew he was taking a risk each time he got behind the wheel, but as months passed without incident, he grew complacent. The 30-mile drive to the construction site each morning soon became just another part of the brothers' daily routine, but this would change on October 14, 2003.

Felipe wasn't feeling well that morning, but he forced himself to get up for work anyway. Apolonia encouraged him to stay home and rest, telling him that missing one day of work wouldn't matter in the long run. He briefly considered it but didn't want to lose a day's pay. He took pride in the fact that he was earning enough money to make sure his wife and three-month-old daughter had everything they needed to live a comfortable life, and he never called out of work. Shrugging off his wife's concerns about his health, he insisted he would be fine. After kissing his wife and daughter goodbye, he hurried out the door.

As usual, it was still dark when Felipe and his brothers climbed into the car to make the 30-mile drive to work. Felipe had made the drive countless times without any problems. But he wasn't feeling well that morning, and it was affecting his concentration. As he came up to the intersection of Immokalee Road and Airport-Pulling Road around 6:30 am, he realized at the last minute that he had inadvertently gotten into the turning lane instead of going straight through the intersection. He tried to make a quick lane change but failed to check for other cars before doing so. As he cut the wheel, he smacked into the side of another car that was already in the straight lane.

Neither car had been traveling at a high rate of

speed, and it was a relatively minor accident. Both cars were still operable, and no one had been injured. The two drivers pulled into the Green Tree Center shopping plaza so they wouldn't be obstructing traffic, then got out of their cars to inspect the damage. The driver of the car Felipe hit was Camille Churchill, and she was calm as she got out of her vehicle. The accident was an inconvenience, but nothing to get angry about. She was somewhat taken aback when Felipe and his brothers got out of their car, as they seemed to be panic-stricken, clearly overreacting to what she could see was just a minor fender-bender.

Unsure of what to do, Camille pulled out her cell phone and called her husband for advice. He told her to call the police to file an accident report. She followed his directions, but this seemed to further agitate the Santos brothers. Frightened due to the fact that they were not in the country legally, they tried to negotiate with Camille, offering to give her cash to compensate for the damage to her car if she would agree not to involve the police. But the three brothers spoke only limited English, and Camille wasn't sure what they were saying. She waved off the handfuls of cash and opted to wait for the police to respond.

A patrol car had been dispatched as soon as Camille had called to report the accident, and Deputy Steven Calkins was on the scene within a few minutes. A 17-year veteran of the Collier County Sheriff's Department, Calkins had a stellar reputation within the agency, and his personnel file was filled with commendations from both supervisors and citizens. While the other driver may have been confused by the agitated state of the Santos brothers, it didn't take the deputy long to ascertain what was going on. Though the accident had been minor, the fact that Felipe was not in the county legally, had no driver's license, and had no insurance elevated the situation to a criminal offense. Deputy Calkins placed Felipe under arrest, charging him with careless driving, driving without a valid driver's license, and having no proof of insurance. In total, the three charges amounted to $2000 in fines and required Felipe to appear in court the following month. He also faced possible deportation back to Mexico.

Witnesses who saw the interaction between Deputy Calkins and Felipe would later describe it as cordial; there had been no raised voices, and no one saw any kind of physical altercation take place. Camille noted that the deputy appeared to be somewhat exasperated at the situation; he commented that he was getting sick of pulling over people who were driving without a valid license, but he remained polite. Nothing was said about Felipe's lack of citizenship. Jorge and Salvador were told they were free to go and were not questioned or detained. All they could do was watch helplessly as Felipe was placed under arrest and put into the back of the patrol car. Deputy Calkins reminded them that they would need to have someone with a valid driver's license retrieve Felipe's car, then drove away.

Salvador and Jorge got a ride to the construction site where they worked and told their boss what was going on. The brothers were understandably upset, and their boss did what he could to calm them down. Knowing that their limited English would be a liability in this situation, he told them that he would call the jail later that afternoon to see what they needed to do to get Felipe out of jail. With luck, they would be able to bail him out that same day, and he would be home before his wife even knew he had been arrested.

After Jorge and Salvador finished work that afternoon, their boss contacted the county jail and explained that he wanted to post bail for Felipe Santos. The operator placed him on hold for a couple of minutes, then came back on the line with the news that no one by that name was in the county jail. Jorge and Salvador were confused. When they last saw Felipe, he had been under arrest and in the back of a patrol car. If he hadn't been taken to jail, where was he?

Knowing that Felipe had been carrying cash when he was arrested, Jorge and Salvador wondered if it was possible that he had been able to bail himself out and head home. It was an optimistic thought, but when they returned to Immokalee there was no sign of Felipe. Though somewhat distressed, the brothers didn't panic at that point. Assuming there was just some kind of mistake, they decided to call the jail again the following morning and hope Felipe had been entered into the system by then. Unfortunately, they got the same answer when they called the jail the next day. Felipe had not been booked into the county jail. Even worse, they were told that no one by that name had even been arrested. There was simply no record of Felipe at all.

Unsure of what had happened to their brother, Jorge and Salvador went to the sheriff's office to see if they could shed any light on the situation. Deputies there confirmed that Felipe had not been arrested, but they could see that he had been issued several citations by Deputy Calkins. When they spoke to the deputy, he said that he had placed Felipe under arrest immediately following the traffic accident. Felipe had been polite and cooperative throughout the encounter, though, so Deputy Calkins decided not to take him to jail. He noted that the citations he had given Felipe carried substantial monetary fines and required him to attend a court hearing. Feeling like this was punishment enough, he let Felipe out at a nearby Circle K gas station. This was about a mile from where Felipe's car had been left.

The deputy said he was worried that Felipe would just get right back behind the wheel if he dropped him off at the car, so he just pulled into the next closest gas station. After reminding Felipe that he would still need to have someone with a valid license come get his car, he let him out of the patrol car. As he drove away, he saw Felipe walking towards the gas station's pay phone and assumed he was calling someone for a ride.

Hearing from Deputy Calkins left the Santos brothers with more questions than answers. They now knew why Felipe wasn't in jail, but they still had no idea where he was. Although the deputy saw Felipe walk towards the pay phone, none of them had received a call from him. While he had been living in the area for a few years, Felipe mostly kept to himself and didn't have a large circle of friends. If he had been in trouble, he would have reached out to his brothers or his wife first, and possibly his boss if he was unable to get ahold of anyone else. But none of them had heard from Felipe, and they were growing increasingly concerned with each hour that passed.

Felipe's family was not content to sit around and wait for him to show up. They decided to do a little investigating on their own to see if they could uncover any clues to Felipe's whereabouts. They started at the Circle K where Deputy Calkins said he left Felipe. They took photographs of the missing man and showed them to some of the employees at the gas station, but no one there recalled seeing Felipe. They found his car in the same spot where Deputy Calkins had left it, but there was nothing to indicate that Felipe had returned to the vehicle since the accident.

After two weeks went by without any word from Felipe, his brothers knew that something was dreadfully wrong. There was no way he would have voluntarily gone this long without getting in touch with someone, and they were certain he would never abandon his wife and daughter like this. Unsure of what else to do, Jorge went to the police on October 29, 2003, and reported his brother missing. The police didn't share their concerns about Felipe's safety and told the family there wasn't much they could do. As an adult, Felipe was free to disappear if he wanted, and there was no evidence leading them to believe that Felipe had met with foul play. They thought it was more likely that Felipe, facing expensive fines and possible deportation, had simply decided to run away from everything and would likely be found in Mexico.

Frustrated with the way local law enforcement had responded, Jorge turned to the Mexican consulate in

Miami for help. While the Mexican government couldn't offer much assistance in the state of Florida's investigation, they started their own search for Felipe in Mexico. The consulate noted that they were normally pretty efficient when it came to locating people, with the majority of the missing located in just two or three weeks. Unfortunately, a check of prisons, hospitals, and morgues failed to turn up any sign of Felipe. There was nothing to indicate that he had made his way back to Mexico, so they assumed that he was most likely still in the United States.

Felipe was due to appear in court on November 24, 2003 on charges stemming from the accident, and when he didn't show up for the hearing a warrant was issued for his arrest. It was the first time he had been in any sort of criminal trouble, and police believed that he deliberately disappeared in order to avoid his court date. His family disagreed. Felipe was close to his family and had been thrilled to become a father three months earlier. He would never have voluntarily abandoned his daughter.

When it became clear that the sheriff's office was not making any attempt to locate Felipe, his brothers decided to force their hand. They filed a formal complaint against Deputy Calkins at the Collier County Sheriff's Department. This forced Internal Affairs to get involved in the investigation, but they were quick to clear Deputy Calkins of any wrongdoing. As far as law enforcement was concerned, there had been no foul play involved in Felipe's disappearance; they considered him to be voluntarily missing. Felipe's wife questioned the thoroughness of their investigation. Her husband had been missing for more than three months, yet she had not been contacted by a single investigator. Considering spouses are usually the first to be suspected when someone goes missing, the fact that no one had asked to speak with her is compelling evidence that law enforcement had never launched an investigation into Felipe's disappearance in the first place.

After a few months of living without her husband, Apolonia decided to leave Immokalee and go back to Oaxaca, Mexico. Law enforcement insisted that Felipe had almost certainly returned to Mexico to avoid facing charges in Florida, but Apolonia knew in her heart that she would not find him there. Although she and Felipe had been planning to move back to their hometown eventually, there was no way he would have gone without her. Still, it made more sense for her to return to her homeland where she would have relatives to help her with her daughter. In February 2004, Apolonia left Florida and went back to Mexico. Jorge and Salvador soon followed. Except for his boss and some coworkers, there was no one left in Florida who had known Felipe, and there was little reason to think that his case would ever be resolved. The case had not attracted any media attention, and the only ones who had actively searched for Felipe had been his own relatives. But before his name could completely fade into obscurity, the January 12, 2004 disappearance of another young man in Florida would propel Felipe's case into national news.

Terrance Williams, a 27-year-old African American man who lived in Naples, Florida, never met Felipe Santos. Terrance had grown up in Chattanooga, Tennessee, and had been living in Florida for around two years when he went missing. He had made the move so he would be closer to his mother, and had initially moved in with her and her new husband. The arrangement didn't last long, as he and his stepfather didn't get along very well. He moved into a house with a roommate but remained close to his mother and phoned her on a daily basis to check in.

Terrance had a somewhat troubled past, but he had been working hard to get his life back on track. While in Tennessee, he had spent time in jail for robbery and had also gotten a DUI. Unfortunately, the DUI conviction resulted in his driver's license being suspended, which made it harder for him to be able to get to work. As a result, Terrance, a father of four, had fallen behind on his child support payments, though he still played an active role in his children's lives. He had made the move to Florida hoping to find a better-paying job so he could get back on track with his child support payments and had been diligent about saving his money.

Terrance returned to Tennessee in October 2003 for a court hearing regarding $5,000 in child support that he still owed, and his next hearing was scheduled for January 14, 2004. Despite the distance between them, he maintained a great relationship with his children. They were a source of pride and joy for him, and they idolized their father. He wanted to make sure they had everything they needed in life and was determined to support them financially.

Terrance, who had long dreadlocks and an open, friendly smile, was known for being extremely fastidious about his appearance. He would even iron his t-shirts before putting them on. While he could be fussy about neatness, he was a hard worker and didn't mind getting his hands dirty. He was employed as a construction worker, and he enjoyed working on cars in his spare time. Although he still had another six months left before he would be able to get his driver's license back, he had a white Cadillac that he had painstakingly restored, and was looking forward to being able to drive again.

Terrance had recently taken a second job as a cook at a Pizza Hut restaurant in Bonita Springs, Florida. This allowed him to put more money away for his child support payments. He was hoping that when he went back to court the judge would be pleased with the progress he had been making, and he was confident that he would soon be completely caught up on his payments.

Since Terrance was prohibited from driving, his mother and his roommate both pitched in to make sure he was able to get to work each day. He worked at Pizza Hut on the afternoon of January 12, 2004, and Marcia picked him up when his shift was over and drove him to his house. He seemed to be in good spirits on the ride home and told his mom that he would talk to her the following day. His roommate, Jason Gonzalez, was already at the house when Terrance arrived. Terrance told him that he had been invited to a small party that night with some of his coworkers from Pizza Hut, and asked Jason if he wanted to come along. Although he was tempted, it was a Sunday night and Jason had to get up early the next morning, so he declined. Terrance was determined to go anyway, seeing it as a good chance for him to get to know his new co-workers in a more relaxed environment. But the party was in Bonita Springs, which was around 20 miles away from his home in East Naples. Since Jason didn't want to go, Terrance couldn't get a ride with him, and he wasn't about to call his mother for a ride late at night. Instead, he made a split-second decision that would have tragic consequences.

Although Terrance had completed restoration work on his Cadillac the previous October, he had yet to drive it. No matter how tempting it may have been, he knew he risked getting into legal trouble if he was caught driving while his license was still suspended. He also had to wait until he got his license back before he could register the car and buy car insurance. Yet for some reason, he decided that night that he was willing to take the risk and drive himself to Bonita Springs. Jason tried to talk him out of it, but Terrance's mind was made up. He assured Jason that he would be extremely careful, and he doubted there would be many patrol cars out there this late on a Sunday night anyway. Jason remained unconvinced, but there wasn't anything he could do to stop his roommate from leaving. All he could do was watch as Terrance grabbed his car keys and walked out the door.

It had been a long time since Terrance had been in a car by himself, so getting behind the wheel must have given him a sense of freedom at first. It didn't take long for reality to set in, however. Terrance hadn't been gone very long when Jason received a call on his cell phone from a number he didn't recognize. It was Terrance, calling him from a payphone. He had seen red and blue flashing lights in his rearview mirror and noticed there were several police cruisers in the area. Panicking, he pulled into the first gas station he saw so he could call his roommate. Although it was clear that the flashing lights had not been directed at him, he thought it was prudent for him to stay off the road for a few minutes just in case. He chatted with Jason for a couple of minutes, then told him that it looked like the cops had cleared out from the area and he felt it was safe for him to drive.

Jason went to bed shortly after talking to Terrance. When he woke up the following morning, he was surprised to see that Terrance wasn't there. He normally kept his cell phone in the bedroom while he slept, but had inadvertently left it in the living room after speaking with Terrance the previous night. Checking it, he saw there were two missed calls from a phone number he wasn't familiar with; both calls had come in around 4:00 am. He called the number back and learned it was a phone belonging to one of Terrance's coworkers. She didn't know why Terrance had tried to call his roommate but told Jason that they had all been having such a good time that the party didn't break up until after dawn. She believed it had been around 6:00 am when Terrance left that morning, and he seemed to be in a good mood. Jason was relieved to know nothing had been wrong and assumed he would see Terrance at some point that day.

Terrance spoke with his mother on an almost daily basis, and while it was unusual for him to go a day without calling, it wasn't necessarily cause for alarm. Yet when Marcia woke up on Monday morning, she couldn't shake the feeling that something was wrong, though she couldn't put her finger on exactly what was making her feel that way. When she didn't hear from Terrance that day, she was unsettled but tried to tell herself she was overreacting. Terrance was an adult, and he was working two jobs. Perhaps he had just been busy with work and unable to call.

Panic didn't set in until the following day, when Jason contacted Marcia to see if she had heard from Terrance. He told her that he hadn't seen Terrance since Sunday night, and had initially assumed he was simply spending some time at his mother's house. When he found out that Terrance had failed to report to work for his scheduled shifts on Monday and Tuesday, he realized something was wrong. Terrance never missed work. Marcia felt her heart sink when Jason told her that Terrance had driven himself to a party in Bonita Springs. She was disappointed that he had chosen to drive with a suspended license, and she was terrified at the thought that he might have been in a car accident, injured and unable to call for help. Jason called everyone he could think of that might have seen Terrance, but no one had any contact with him after he left the party early Monday morning.

Desperate to find her son, Marcia drove to the Collier County Sheriff's Office North Naples substation and tried to file a missing persons report. No one there seemed at all concerned, telling her that Terrance was an adult, free to come and go as he pleased. It was the same response Jorge and Salvador Santos had gotten three months before when they tried to report their brother missing. Like the Santos family, Marica quickly reached the conclusion that she couldn't count on the police to investigate her son's disappearance. It looked like the only way Terrance was going to be found was if she went out there and found him herself.

One of the first calls Marica made was to the Tennessee home of Terrance's four children. It was a heartbreaking call to make. Keiaira, his oldest child and the only girl, took the news particularly hard. She had been especially close to her father and considered him to be one of her best friends. Her three brothers were too young at the time to fully grasp what was going on, but they missed their dad and couldn't understand why the police were unable to find him. All Marcia could do was reassure her grandchildren that she was doing everything possible to find their beloved dad.

Marcia was the only one of Terrance's family members who was living in Florida, and the majority of the relatives were in Tennessee. While they couldn't physically search for Terrance, they quickly began working the phones, placing calls to prisons and hospitals in Florida, hoping that someone would be able to tell them where Terrance was. It was a tedious process. After spending a couple of days calling every place they could think of, the family was starting to get discouraged. Finally, on January 16th, they got a break: Marcia's sister had managed to locate Terrance's car. A towing company she called told her that they did indeed have the white Cadillac in their lot, and it had been there for several days. She quickly called Marcia with the news. Finally, they had uncovered a tangible piece of evidence that might help them locate Terrance. It was what Marcia had been hoping for, but at the same time, the news filled her with dread as she was unsure what they would find inside the car.

According to the towing company, the Cadillac had been towed to their yard on January 12th after being found abandoned near Hodges Funeral Home at the Naples Memorial Garden cemetery. Marica immediately called the Collier County Sheriff's office with the news that Terrance's car had been located. She couldn't shake the fear that her son's body could possibly be in the trunk of his own car, and she asked if a deputy could be sent to examine the Cadillac. While some of Terrance's belongings were found inside the car, there was no sign of Terrance. There was no body damage to the car, so it didn't appear that an accident had occurred. There was no blood or anything else to indicate that something had happened to Terrance while he was in the car. Though relieved that Terrance's body hadn't been found in his car, his family still had no answers about where he was.

Marcia decided to take a drive to the location where the Cadillac had been found. When she got there, she saw several cemetery employees working on the grounds. The chances any of them had witnessed something relevant to Terrance's disappearance seemed slim, but Marcia approached them anyway. Her persistence paid off. The men had indeed seen Terrance and his white Cadillac that Monday morning, and what they told Marcia would change the course of the investigation.

While Terrance had managed to successfully avoid getting pulled over on his way to the party Sunday night, his luck ran out on Monday morning. As he was driving past the cemetery, he was pulled over. The cemetery employees were not close enough to hear anything Terrance or the deputy were saying, but they said it appeared to be a civil conversation. After a couple of minutes, Terrance got into the back seat of the patrol car, but he wasn't handcuffed, and the men couldn't tell if he had been placed under arrest or not. The deputy drove off, but returned about 45 minutes later without Terrance. It was at that point that he called and arranged to have the Cadillac towed from the cemetery parking lot. The deputy left after that, and the cemetery employees did not see him or Terrance again.

When the men told Marcia what they had seen, she was relieved at first. Terrance had taken a big risk when he decided to drive with a suspended license, and it clearly hadn't worked out for him. Combined with the fact that the Cadillac was unregistered, and Terrance had no car insurance, it made sense that Terrance had been arrested after getting pulled over. Although Marcia had been told that there was no record of Terrance being booked into jail, she assumed it must have been an oversight. Thanks to the paperwork kept by the towing company, Marcia now had the name of the deputy that had called to have Terrance's car towed. Armed with this new information, Marcia called the sheriff's department. To her surprise, they still claimed that Terrance hadn't been arrested by any of their deputies. Marcia insisted on talking to the deputy who had towed her son's car but was told that it was his day off. Marcia persisted until the dispatcher finally decided to call the deputy at home to see if he could shed any light on the situation.

When the dispatcher called him, the deputy insisted that he hadn't arrested anyone on Monday, and he didn't recall having a Cadillac towed either. The dispatcher was inclined to believe him. He was a long-time veteran of the force and had an impeccable record. Still, he was the last person known to talk to the missing man, so he understood why he was being questioned. He wasn't particularly worried, as he had been in a similar situation before. Just a few days earlier, an internal investigation had cleared him of any wrongdoing in the case of another missing man. The deputy was Steven Calkins, the last known person to have been with Felipe Santos before he went missing three months earlier.

When she learned that the deputy was claiming to have no memory of her son or his car, Marcia was confused. It had only been four days, and it was hard for her to believe that an experienced deputy like Calkins could forget something like that so quickly. Had she known about the connection between Deputy Calkins and Felipe Santos, she would have been stunned and demanded answers. But Felipe's case had never been covered by the news media, so Marcia – and the rest of the state – had no knowledge about it. Giving the deputy the benefit of the doubt, Marcia wondered if the cemetery workers were somehow mistaken about what they saw.

Trying desperately to turn up some new leads, Terrance's friends and family had missing flyers printed and began handing them out to everyone they saw. They were hoping that their constant presence on the streets of Naples would pressure the sheriff's department to look into Terrance's disappearance, and they were eventually successful. But when they finally opened a missing persons case on Terrance, detectives immediately picked up on his troubled past. In addition to serving time in prison for robbery and having a suspended license because of his

DUI, Terrance had two social security numbers and two dates of birth that he would use interchangeably when interacting with law enforcement. This was an immediate red flag to investigators because there was no legal reason for a person to do this. He had also missed his court date in Tennessee, and there had been a warrant issued for his arrest in Hamilton County. The detectives felt that the warrant alone was reason enough for Terrance to voluntarily disappear, and if he was using false information, he was likely to try to go underground and start a new life elsewhere. As an adult, he had the right to disappear if that's what he wanted, and police seemed to believe it would be a waste of time looking for someone who didn't want to be found.

Friends and family disputed the police contention that Terrance had voluntarily disappeared. They pointed out that the warrant in Hamilton County, Tennessee had only been issued after Terrance missed his January 14th court date. This was two days after he disappeared. He would never have willingly skipped out on the child support hearing; up until this point, he had been diligent about attending all of his court dates. They also pointed out that Terrance had a paycheck waiting for him at the time he went missing, and it was unlikely he would have gone anywhere without picking it up.

As Marcia continued her own investigation into her son's disappearance, she found it hard to get past the fact that the cemetery workers were positive they had seen Terrance get into the back seat of a police car. She wasn't about to let the matter drop just because Deputy Calkins insisted he had not had any encounters with Terrance. She was determined to find her son and continued to call the sheriff's office to demand answers.

Although none of Terrance's family members were aware of the parallels between his disappearance and that of Felipe Santos, the Collier County Sheriff's Department certainly was, and they were troubled by it. Though Deputy Calkins had told the police dispatcher that he had no recollection of dealing with Terrance or his car, the department knew they needed to take a closer look at the case. On January 19th, a week after Terrance went missing, Deputy Calkins met with his supervisor to discuss the incident. Having had some time to think about it, the deputy now claimed that he did remember having a brief encounter with Terrance, and his supervisor asked him to submit a written incident report about it.

According to Deputy Calkins, he had been out on routine patrol when he saw a motorist in a white Cadillac who appeared to be having some kind of mechanical trouble. He motioned for the driver to pull over, and the driver pulled into the cemetery parking lot. The driver of the vehicle told Deputy Calkins that his car wasn't running right and he was afraid he was going to be late for work and lose his job as a result. The deputy offered to call a cab for him, but the driver said he couldn't afford one. Deputy Calkins stated that the driver then asked him if he could give him a ride to work, claiming he worked at the Circle K on Wiggins Pass Road, and the deputy agreed to do so. He asked the cemetery employees if it was okay to leave the Cadillac there until he could arrange to have it towed, and they told him that was fine. He said he would return after dropping the driver off at work.

Deputy Calkin told his supervisor that the interaction had been so short that he only got the driver's first name: Terrance. As he dropped him off at the Circle K, Deputy Calkins warned Terrance that his car had an expired tag, but Terrance assured him that he had already taken care of it. He said that both the receipt and the proper registration papers could be found in the car's glove compartment. Deputy Calkins said he believed Terrance was telling the truth but soon found out otherwise.

After leaving Terrance at the Circle K, Deputy Calkins returned to the Cadillac. Before he called dispatch to have the car towed, he checked the glove compartment and discovered it was empty. In the incident report, he noted "I now felt that Terrance had deceived me. I called for a wrecker, thinking that the Cadillac was abandoned or maybe even stolen." He then called the Circle K and asked to speak to Terrance, but was told no one by that name worked there. He admitted that he had been angry about being lied to, but assured his supervisors that he had no further interaction with Terrance, and that he had no idea what had happened to him after he left the Circle K.

When Marcia learned Deputy Calkin's version of events, she immediately knew something was wrong. She didn't believe that Terrance would have ever asked a police officer to drive him anywhere. He had no love for law enforcement officers and would have tried to get a ride with her or one of his friends if he needed one. She also disputed the deputy's statement about the Cadillac not running right, insisting that it had been in perfect shape and she had been able to drive it home from the towing yard without any problems. Surveillance footage from security cameras at the Circle K was scrutinized, but there was no sign of Terrance or Deputy Calkins on the day in question.

Frustrated, Marcia and her husband filed a misconduct complaint against Deputy Calkins and the Collier County Sheriff's Department. They did not believe it was possible that Deputy Calkins would have simply let Terrance go without even issuing him a citation. He had no valid driver's license, his car wasn't registered, and he had no car insurance. They were also troubled by the fact that Deputy Calkins hadn't been asked to provide a written incident report until a week after Terrance went missing.

Marcia wasn't the only person questioning what had really gone on that day. Investigators had listened to the dispatch recording from when Deputy Calkins had arranged to have the Cadillac towed, and they realized that there were several inconsistencies between what they heard on the recording and the information contained in the deputy's incident report. Deputy Calkins told the dispatcher that he had come across the Cadillac blocking part of the road in front of the cemetery, and that there was no one around. He said he believed the car had either been abandoned there or was stolen, and arranged to have it towed. This happened after he claimed he took Terrance to the Circle K, so he certainly knew that the car hadn't been abandoned. There was no evidence to back up his claim that the Cadillac had been obstructing traffic, either. The cemetery workers who witnessed the incident told investigators that the Cadillac had initially been parked in the cemetery parking lot, not in the road. When

Deputy Calkins returned from the Circle K, he moved the car and parked it on the roadway. Inconsistencies alone didn't prove that the deputy was a murderer, but it was clear he had been lying about the encounter from the beginning, at least to the dispatcher. Especially disturbing to his supervisors was the fact that this dispatcher and Deputy Calkins were good friends. The fact that he was lying to a close friend raised a lot of red flags and convinced the investigators that the deputy was hiding something.

Deputy Calkins was asked to submit to a polygraph concerning Terrance's disappearance, and he agreed. He was asked if he had dropped Terrance off at the Circle K that day, and he said that he had. He was also asked if he had taken Terrance anywhere other than the Circle K, and he said he had not. He passed the test.

Marcia had trouble believing the deputy had passed the polygraph, and she worried that this would mean detectives would stop looking for her son. She decided to get the news media involved. The Naples Daily News ran a short article about Terrance's disappearance, asking the public to keep an eye out for him and to call if they had any information about his whereabouts. Not long after the first article was published, Marcia received a phone call that changed everything. The case had attracted the attention of the Mexican consulate in Miami. They were curious to know if Marcia had been aware of Felipe Santos, who had gone missing under eerily similar circumstances just three miles from the cemetery where Terrance was last seen. It was the first time Marcia had heard Felipe's name, but it wouldn't be the last. The parallels between the two cases were disturbing, and couldn't be ignored.

Though Deputy Calkins had passed a polygraph, the fact that he was the last person to see two different people immediately before they went missing could not be ignored and needed to be investigated. In order to avoid any potential conflicts of interest, the Collier County Sheriff's Department wisely asked several outside agencies to take over the investigation. Going forward, the case would be in the hands of the Florida Department of Law Enforcement, the FBI, and the State Attorney's office.

As the investigation progressed, detectives found several other inconsistencies between dispatch recordings and the incident report Deputy Calkins had written. The deputy told his supervisors that he had never gotten Terrance's last name during the encounter, but after he called in to have the car towed, he placed another call to dispatch and asked for a background check on a Terrance Williams with a birthdate of 4-1-1975. Going by the timeline provided in his written statement, Deputy Calkins had already dropped Terrance off at this point. There was no paperwork in the Cadillac with Terrance's last name on it, so Terrance must have told the deputy his full name. Further complicating the matter, the birthdate called in by Calkins was not Terrance's correct birthdate. It was the fake one that he had used in the past when trying to trick police. There was no way Deputy Calkins could have known this date unless Terrance himself had provided it to him.

Deputy Calkins maintained that he had used his Nextel to call the Circle K after he realized there was no paperwork in the glove compartment of the Cadillac. He said he had gotten the phone number out of the phone book that was kept in the patrol car. Yet when his phone records were examined, they showed no calls made to the Circle K, and none of the employees there recalled speaking to the deputy. Furthermore, the phone number for this particular Circle K wasn't even listed in the phone book Deputy Calkins said he used.

As their investigation continued, detectives administered another polygraph examination to Calkins, this time concentrating on the numerous inconsistencies in his story. When asked if Terrance had been in the car with him when he phoned dispatch to get a background check done, his "no" answer indicated deception. He was also deemed to be lying when he said that he had no contact with Terrance after dropping him off at the Circle K. The examiner concluded that the deputy was not being truthful and told him he failed the polygraph. Unable to provide an explanation for the numerous inconsistencies and sensing that the detectives were turning against him, Calkins grew frustrated. He accused the investigators of waging a politically motivated attack against him because it was an election year and the sheriff was up for reelection. When the detectives pointed out that it would do the sheriff more harm than good to have one of his deputies fail a lie detector exam, Deputy Calkins simply stopped cooperating with them and left the station. He retained a lawyer and refused to speak with the investigators again.

While the failed polygraph elevated Deputy Calkins to prime suspect status in the eyes of many, detectives had been unable to show that a crime had actually been committed. Circumstantial evidence was piling up, but they had no physical evidence suggesting that Calkins had harmed either of the missing men. An extensive forensic investigation was conducted on the deputy's patrol car, but it yielded nothing. The car had been very well-maintained, and it didn't look like anything violent had occurred in it. A GPS device was surreptitiously placed on the patrol car, and investigators monitored it to see if they could pinpoint any isolated areas that Deputy Calkins might have frequented while out on patrol. Once again, they came up empty-handed.

There had never been any large-scale searches for Felipe or Terrance when they first went missing, but this changed in the spring of 2004. Investigators combed through miles of wetlands and other remote areas within Collier County, even going as far as dragging some of the lakes in the area. They deployed cadaver dogs in places that were part of Deputy Calkin's normal patrol routine and used helicopters to fly over marshy areas looking for anything unusual. Detectives were sent out to interview anyone who had any kind of contact with the deputy, from coworkers and neighbors to friends and acquaintances of his wife. Not a single person they spoke with believed that Deputy Calkins had anything to do with the two disappearances.

After months of careful investigation, detectives were unable to find any evidence that Deputy Calkins had harmed either of the missing men. They knew he hadn't been truthful in some of his earlier statements about what had happened, but that alone wasn't enough to charge him with murder. He had lied and tried to mislead investigators, though, and the sheriff could no longer trust him to faithfully uphold his oath to serve and protect the people of Collier County. In August 2004, Deputy Calkins was fired due to violation of agency procedures and policies. He appealed, but Sheriff Don Hunter upheld the termination. Even after Deputy Calkins was fired, the sheriff's office continued to maintain that there was no evidence indicating that Felipe and Terrance were no longer alive. The cases were still treated as missing person cases, not as homicide investigations.

There were many people in Collier County who still supported Calkins and didn't believe he had done anything wrong, and they questioned why he had been terminated from the police force. They pointed out that Calkins had no obvious motive to kill either man, and each man had been stopped in broad daylight in a populated area where there were numerous witnesses to the encounter. No one had seen any kind of argument or physical altercation take place; all the witnesses who came forward noted that the deputy's interactions with each man appeared to be perfectly pleasant.

The fact that Deputy Calkins lost his job meant little to Terrance's family. They still didn't know what had happened to him. Felipe's family was in the same position. Years went by, and the missing men seemed to be forgotten by everyone except their loved ones. This changed in 2012 when Trayvon Martin, an unarmed black teenager, was shot and killed in Miami Springs, Florida. The case had captivated the nation, and civil rights activists used the publicity Trayvon's case had attracted to draw attention to other unsolved cases involving minorities. Tyler Perry, a well-known actor and director, had been watching television coverage about Trayvon when he heard someone mention the two missing men from the Naples area. He had never heard of either missing man before, so he did a little research on the case. What he learned horrified and appalled him. It was hard to believe that two men could vanish under nearly identical circumstances that seemed to point directly to the person responsible, yet nothing had been done. He felt compelled to get involved.

For years, Marcia had been fighting a lonely battle to get justice for her son. Suddenly, she had the support of an A-list celebrity, and Terrance's case was making headlines across the nation. In January 2013, Tyler Perry, Rev. Al Sharpton, and NAACP President Ben Jealous held a press conference in Naples. Marcia was at Tyler's side when he announced that he was offering a $100,000 reward for information about the disappearances of Felipe and Terrance. Although numerous tips were called in, none shed any light on the strange disappearances.

In August 2018, civil rights attorney Ben Crump filed a wrongful death suit against Steven Calkins, who had long since left Florida but remained a person of interest in the case. The lawsuit alleged that Terrance Williams was dead, and Calkins was responsible for his death. Felipe's family was not a party to the litigation. Crump was hopeful that evidence presented in the civil lawsuit would later lead to a criminal case against the former deputy. At the same time, Tyler Perry announced that he was doubling the reward offered in the case to $200,000, hoping that the large cash reward would entice anyone who had information on the case to finally come forward and tell police what they knew.

As expected, Steven Calkins filed a motion to dismiss the wrongful death case, but this motion was denied in February 2019. He appealed, arguing that a statute of limitations for wrongful death complaints alleging murder and manslaughter applied to his case. On June 5, 2019, a judge reversed the earlier decision and granted the motion to dismiss.

Felipe Santos and Terrance Williams have never been found, and with the dismissal of the civil lawsuit against Steven Calkins, it's possible that their families might never know the truth about what happened to the two men. Numerous theories have been put forth, but without evidence to confirm or reject any particular theory, it has been impossible for detectives to close the case. Some believe that Steven Calkins killed both men, but investigators have continuously stressed the fact that there is absolutely no physical evidence suggesting that Felipe and Terrance are dead. No bodies have been found, and no crime scene has been identified. Both men had reasons why they might have wanted to run away and start over somewhere else. Both were actively breaking the law when they encountered Calkins. Terrance was facing possible jail time in Tennessee, and Felipe was facing deportation. But each man also had very close family ties that make it seem unlikely that they simply walked away.

It's impossible to ignore the similarities between the two cases. Perhaps Tyler Perry put it best: when he was asked if it was possible that Steven Calkins was innocent, he said that if Calkins was innocent, he was the unluckiest man in the world. He was the last known person to have contact with each man before they went missing, a coincidence that defies probability. Each man vanished shortly after they were seen being put in his police car, and he wasn't entirely truthful about his encounters with the two men. He certainly seems like the obvious suspect. Yet he had been a deputy for 17 years without incident. No one had anything bad to say about him. If he was a murderer, he managed to keep that aspect of his personality completely hidden from everyone around him. It's hard to believe that he suddenly became a serial killer at the age of 50.

It's possible that the truth about what happened to the two men lies somewhere in the middle. Some believe that Deputy Calkins didn't actually kill either of the men, but facilitated their death. In 2000, several Aboriginal men were found dead from hypothermia in Saskatoon, Saskatchewan. At least one of the men had last been seen in the back of a police car, and their deaths were allegedly caused by members of the Saskatoon Police Force. The SPF was accused of arresting Aboriginal people for minor offenses and then, instead of taking them to jail, driving them to the outskirts of town and leaving them there in the frigid night air. The lucky ones managed to find a way to get back to town. The unlucky ones froze to death. These so-called "Starlight Tours" had allegedly been going on for decades; there is evidence that the practice had begun in 1976. Some people have suggested that Terrance and Felipe met a similar fate. While they wouldn't have to worry about hypothermia in Florida, if they had been abandoned in the Everglades there were many other dangers that could have killed them. Though it makes for a convenient explanation, there is absolutely no evidence to suggest that this practice ever went on in the state of Florida.

Both Felipe Santos and Terrance Williams remain listed as missing persons. Detectives still receive occasional tips about possible sightings of the men, and they continue to investigate all leads that come in. They believe someone knows what happened to the two men, and are hopeful they will one day get the information needed to solve the case.

Felipe Maximino Santos was 23 years old when he disappeared from Naples, Florida in October 2003. He was a new father who was devoted to his wife and daughter. Felipe has brown eyes and black hair, and at the time of his disappearance, he was 5 feet 7 inches tall and weighed 150 pounds. When last seen, he was wearing a t-shirt, jeans, and a pair of work boots, and spoke only limited English.

Terrance Deon Williams was 27 years old when he disappeared from Naples, Florida in January 2004. He had four children he was deeply devoted to and was very close to his mother. Felipe has brown eyes and brown hair worn in dreadlocks. At the time of his disappearance, he was 5 feet 8 inches tall and weighed 160 pounds. He had three tattoos: the letter T on the upper left side of his chest, the initials ET on his right shoulder, and "Terrance" on his left forearm. He had a gold crown with the letter T on his upper right front tooth, and a solid gold crown on his upper left front tooth. He had a vertical scar on his right shoulder and a dark birthmark on the right side of his abdomen. When last seen, he was wearing a short-sleeved shirt with buttons down the front, blue jeans, and Timberland boots. He was also wearing diamond earrings and a watch with a silver band.

If you have any information about Felipe or Terrance, please call the Collier County Sheriff's Department at 239-252-9300.

Nefertiri Trader

Nefertiri Trader, a 33-year-old mother of three, decided to take a late-night drive to a convenience store on June 30, 2014. There was a 7-11 store a few minutes away from her home in the Saddlebrook neighborhood of New Castle, Delaware, and Nefertiri — called Neffie by her friends — was a regular there. Neffie had been living in her Saddlebrook home for nearly a decade and often went to the 7-11 late at night to get coffee or cigarettes. She was currently on medical leave from her job at Christiana Hospital and tended to stay up until the wee hours of the morning.

It was sometime around 3:30 am when she decided to go to the 7-11 on this particular night. She made the drive there and back without incident. It's unclear exactly what happened after she parked her car in her driveway, but her family does not believe she ever made it back inside her home.

Joe Robinson, who lived across the street from Neffie, woke up at 4:00 am when he heard what he thought was a scream. He looked out of the window in his second-floor bedroom and noticed that Neffie's porch light was on, illuminating her front lawn. He could see a man who appeared to be dragging a woman across the lawn; the man then put the woman in the back seat of Neffie's car. Joe wasn't sure exactly what was going on, so he decided to go outside and see if anyone needed help. By the time he made his way downstairs and went out his front door, the car had already driven away. Neither Neffie nor her car were ever seen again.

Joe briefly considered calling police, but didn't really want to get involved because he had no real knowledge of the situation. He went back inside and returned to bed. He would later tell authorities that he assumed the woman was simply sick and the man was taking her to the hospital. It was an assumption he would regret for years to come.

Denise Trader, Neffie's mother, placed several calls to her daughter throughout the day but was unable to reach her. At 6:00 pm, she decided to drive over to Neffie's house to make sure she was okay. When she got there, Neffie's car was not in the driveway. On the lawn, she found a loaf of bread that looked as if someone had stepped on it. Denise also noticed a cup of coffee, a pack of cigarettes, and a single unopened condom placed on a porch chair. A pair of flip-flops, later determined to be Neffie's, were located next to the front door. There was no sign of Neffie inside the house. Denise immediately called the police and reported her daughter missing.

New Castle County Police conducted a canvass of the neighborhood trying to find anyone who had information about Neffie. When they knocked on Joe Robinson's door and explained why they were there, his heart sank. He told them about what he had seen the previous night and recalled that the man had been wearing a dark hooded sweatshirt and tan shorts. Unfortunately, he didn't really get a good look at the man so was unable to provide a description of his physical characteristics.

Since it appeared Neffie had been taken away in her own vehicle, police issued a description of the car and asked patrol officers to keep an eye out for it. It was a silver 2000 Acura CL with Delaware license plate number

404893. Unfortunately, more than 16 hours had gone by between the time Neffie was abducted and the time police were notified, and there were no reported sightings of her or her car. They could have been just about anywhere along the east coast by that point.

Other than what the neighbor had observed, there were very few clues pointing to what had happened. The smashed loaf of bread located in the front yard suggested that some kind of struggle had taken place there; it appears that Neffie was approached by someone shortly after she got out of her car. Her shoes and other belongings found on the porch seem to indicate that she never made it into the house.

Neffie's case received very little media attention, and few tips were called in to police. Three months into their investigation, detectives admitted that they had no strong leads and had not been able to develop any solid information about the abduction. They could see no apparent reason why anyone would target Neffie, and none of their usual confidential informants had heard any whispers about the case. The investigation was at a standstill from almost the first day.

Denise Trader was absolutely devastated by her daughter's disappearance and was unable to concentrate on anything else. She spent hours driving around Delaware, scanning the streets in search of Neffie or her car. She refused to entertain the idea that Neffie had been killed; she was confident that her daughter was still alive and waiting to be found.

Denise spoke with dozens of people who had known her daughter. She carried a spiral notebook with her at all times, and would carefully take down notes on each conversation. Unable to sleep, she constantly paged through her notes, looking desperately for any clue that might lead to Neffie.

In February 2015, the New Castle County Police started offering $10,000 rewards for information about some of their unsolved cases, including Neffie's. Denise was hopeful that the prospect of financial gain might entice someone with knowledge about what happened to Neffie to finally come forward. Police did receive a few tips, but they led only to dead ends.

February was usually a happy time for the Trader family, as Neffie and her mother shared a February birthday. The entire family would usually gather at Denise's house for a joint birthday party, but they had little to celebrate this year. Denise couldn't bring herself to celebrate her own birthday while her daughter was still missing. She spent the day praying that Neffie would soon be home where she belonged. Hoping to raise money so a larger reward could be offered, she started selling bracelets. It was somewhat bittersweet, as it was a hobby that Neffie herself had once enjoyed.

In June 2015, the New Castle County Police and the FBI held a news conference regarding Neffie's abduction. They announced that new rewards were being offered in the case; $10,000 from New Castle County and $20,000 from the FBI. Both agencies believed that there were people in the area who knew exactly what had happened to Neffie, and they urged them to come forward with this information. Police have been hindered by the fact that many of the people they believe have knowledge of the case refuse to speak with law enforcement, and the investigation has suffered because of this code of silence.

The FBI arranged to install billboards at various locations along Interstate 95 between Maryland and Connecticut. The billboards, which contained information about the case and the reward, urged anyone with knowledge of the case to call the FBI.

Denise Trader also attended the news conference, and she pleaded with the public to help her find her daughter. Although she forced herself to stay strong for the sake of Neffie's three children – she was now raising them – she admitted that she thought about Neffie constantly and just wanted to be able to bring her home.

Both the New Castle County police and the FBI have been convinced from the beginning that Neffie was the victim of foul play, abducted by force from her own property. In 2017, however, the FBI went a step further and stated that they presumed she was deceased.

Neffie's abduction is troubling because of the lack of information available. She was taken by force from her own front yard, and police have never been able to determine a motive for the crime. The fact that there was an unopened condom found on the porch has led some to speculate that she may have known her abductor, perhaps even invited him over, and something went wrong. If she did invite someone over, that person has never been identified.

The fact that she was forced into her own car seems to indicate that her abductor did not have his own vehicle there. Public transportation does not run that late at night, so he would have had to walk there or get a ride with someone else. It's possible Neffie picked him up herself, though she was alone when seen on surveillance video at the 7-11 that night. No one has come forward to admit giving anyone a ride to Neffie's home that day.

Although authorities believe that Neffie is deceased, Denise has continued to hold onto the hope that her daughter is still alive somewhere. She is still actively searching for Neffie, and will not stop until she finds her. If Neffie could have been found using sheer willpower alone, Denise would have brought her home already.

Nefertiri Trader was 33 years old when she went missing in 2014. She has brown eyes and brown hair, and at the time of her disappearance, she was 5 feet 6 inches tall and weighed 125 pounds. She has tattoos on her lower back, left arm, and right chest, and had a scar on her left leg. She was last seen wearing a pink sweatsuit. Her car, a silver 2000 Acura CL with Delaware license plate 404893 is also missing. If you have any information about Neffie or her car, please contact the FBI Baltimore office at 410-265-8080 or New Castle County Cold Case Squad Detective Brian Shahan at 302-395-2781. You can also email Detective Shahan at BShahan@nccde.org.

Daffany Tullos

Daffany Tullos lived with her grandparents, John and Shirley Tullos, in Jackson, Mississippi, but her mother lived nearby and she saw her often. Her mother, Robbie Tullos stopped by the house on the evening of July 26, 1988, and was in the process of making fish sticks for her 2-year-old twins when she got into an argument with Daffany. The 7-year-old told her mother she was hungry and wanted some fish sticks, too; Robbie Tullos told her daughter that she already had dinner and didn't need to eat anything else. After arguing for a couple of minutes, Robbie gave in and handed Daffany a fish stick, but the child was still angry. She took the fish stick and stalked out the front door.

Robbie assumed Daffany was just going to stay in the front yard, as she didn't bother to put any shoes on before she left the house. It was after 7:00 pm, but it was still light out and Daffany knew that she was allowed to play outside until it got dark. Some of her friends saw her walking away from her home in the 4400 block of Azalea Circle in the direction of Northside Drive.

It started to get dark shortly after 8:00 pm, but Daffany didn't return home. Robbie went outside and looked for her, but Daffany was nowhere to be seen. After searching on her own for a short period of time, she started to panic and called the Jackson Police Department.

It was clear that Daffany had left her home voluntarily, but she had not told anyone where she was going and no one was sure how far she had actually walked. Her friends had seen her heading towards Northside Drive, which intersected Azalea Circle about four blocks away from Daffany's house. They were unable to tell if she had continued walking all the way to the intersection; it was possible she changed course or stopped somewhere along the way.

Although there was nothing to indicate that foul play had taken place, police were concerned because of Daffany's young age. They immediately conducted a search of the area, expecting to find Daffany hiding somewhere, perhaps still sulking because of the fish stick incident. After they searched for a few hours without finding any sign of the child, they began to worry that the situation was more serious than they initially thought.

Daffany had been diagnosed with epilepsy and was on several medications to prevent her from having seizures. If she didn't take them as prescribed each day, she was at risk for adverse withdrawal effects and worsening seizures. Police realized that it was extremely important that she be located as soon as possible.

After 72 hours of non-stop searching, police were at a loss. Their search had covered a six-block radius around Daffany's Azalea Court home, but they hadn't located any clues pointing to her whereabouts. Although they had not found any evidence of foul play, they were certain that Daffany had been abducted.

Investigators canvassed the area again on July 29, 1988, going door-to-door throughout the neighborhood handing out flyers describing the missing child. They told residents that they were offering a $2,500 reward for information leading to the location of Daffany, but no one in the area had seen or heard anything useful to the investigation.

Investigators tracked down Daffany's biological dad

and interviewed him; he had never been a part of Daffany's life and did not live in Jackson. They were able to quickly clear him of any involvement in the child's disappearance.

According to Daffany's grandmother, Shirley Tullos, Daffany was afraid of the dark and would never stay out after the sun went down. Although they had initially hoped that Daffany had gone off to hide at a friend's house for the night after the argument with her mother, they knew in their hearts that she simply wasn't the kind of child who would do that. She was well aware of the consequences of skipping doses of her medication, and she never would have voluntarily done so.

There were numerous tips called in to both police and Daffany's family during the first few days of the investigation, and investigators followed up on each one. Several people called in to say they had seen the missing girl, but none of the sightings could be confirmed. One woman was confident she had seen Daffany leaving a park with an unknown male; the child seemed quite upset and appeared to be crying.

Detectives looked into the woman's claim and were able to identify the man and the child she had seen. They confirmed that the girl wasn't Daffany, although she looked enough like her that they could have been sisters. The man seen with her was her father; he explained that she had been crying because she didn't want to stop playing when it was time to leave the park and go home.

The case took a sinister turn when detectives learned that Daffany had recently accused her mother's boyfriend of sexually abusing her. Daffany had spent the night at her mother's Bailey Avenue apartment on June 29, 1988; she later told her aunt that she woke up in the middle of the night and Ernest Lee Epps was fondling her.

Her aunt went to the police and told them what had happened, and they interviewed Ernest. Although he maintained his innocence, he was arrested on charges of sexual battery against the child on July 8th. He was released after paying a $1,000 bond on the morning of July 26th; Daffany went missing that evening.

Detectives believed it was possible that Ernest had done something to Daffany so that police would be forced to drop the sexual battery case, but they were unable to find any evidence linking him to her disappearance. He remained a person of interest, however, and investigators continued working hard to determine what had happened to the missing girl.

Robbie insisted that Ernest, who was the father of her two-year-old twins, had always acted appropriately around the children and she did not believe he would be capable of doing anything to Daffany. She was asked to submit to a polygraph, and agreed; she later told the news media that she failed the test because she was still too emotional over Daffany's disappearance. Police would not confirm or deny her claim.

Ernest remained a person of interest, and Shirley Tullos believed it was possible he had done something to her granddaughter. She told police that his family had tried to offer her $175 to drop the sexual battery claim against Ernest, but she had refused. Now, she worried that Daffany's disappearance had resulted from this refusal.

Not long after Daffany went missing, Robbie reported to police that someone had called her and told her to bring $5,000 to a specific address and the caller would tell her where she could find her daughter. Detectives were immediately dispatched to that address, where they found an elderly couple who had absolutely no idea what the detectives were doing there. The couple, as well as Daffany's family, had been the victims of a cruel hoax.

Two weeks into the investigation, authorities acknowledged that the situation was dire. If Daffany were still alive, she had been without her medication for so long that it was possible she could die from a seizure. Although the family still held onto the hope that she would be found alive, detectives had their doubts. They had exhausted all available leads but were unable to find any evidence pointing to any one suspect.

John and Shirley, who had essentially raised Daffany since birth, were devastated by her disappearance. A month after their granddaughter vanished, they admitted to reporters that they believed the pending sexual assault case was connected to Daffany's disappearance. They refused to believe that Robbie had any knowledge of what had happened to her; they acknowledged that she appeared blinded by her love for Ernest, but they were adamant that she would never be involved in harming her child.

Robbie told reporters that she didn't understand why police thought she knew more than she was telling them. She was aware that they seemed to be focusing on her – she had been interviewed on numerous occasions – but she insisted that she was as in the dark as the rest of the family. She admitted that it seemed strange that her daughter went missing the same day Ernest bonded out of jail, but she still didn't think he had anything to do with Daffany's disappearance.

Five months after Daffany went missing, a woman came forward with a potential tip that sent investigators scrambling to a field to the west of Jackson. The caller claimed that she and her boyfriend had witnessed an unidentified man dump a young girl's body in the field around the time Daffany disappeared. Although it was unclear why the couple waited so long to come forward with this information, it was the first tip detectives had received in weeks and they immediately followed up with the woman and her boyfriend.

The couple claimed that they had witnessed a man carry a child into the field, then return a few minutes later by himself. Despite the fact that they believed he had dumped the child there, they didn't call police and they didn't venture into the field themselves. Investigators spent hours combing through the 15-acre field, hoping that this was the break they needed to solve the case. Unfortunately, they found nothing to indicate that a body had been dumped there.

In February 1990, Daffany's grandmother was helping one of her neighbors hang some laundry on the clothesline in her backyard. At one point, the pair noticed a sweatshirt in a nearby yard and went over to pick it up. It was very dirty and had apparently been outside for a long period of time; upon closer inspection, Shirley realized that it was her granddaughter's sweatshirt. Daffany's name had been written on the tag in marker and was still partially visible.

The ladies immediately called police to report the find, and detectives took the sweatshirt to be processed for evidence, but they didn't believe it had anything to do with the child's disappearance. It had been summer when Daffany went missing and she had been wearing only shorts and a sleeveless shirt; it was possible she had left the sweatshirt outside long before she had gone missing. No one could recall if she had lent the sweatshirt to a friend or a cousin; she may not have been the last person to wear it.

Detectives questioned the residents of the

property where the sweatshirt was found, but none of them were able to offer any insight on how it got there. No forensic evidence was found on the shirt when it was processed, and police determined that the sweatshirt's appearance was likely a freak coincidence.

In both 1991 and 1992, Daffany's photograph was included on the cover of a political questionnaire that was sent out by Senator Trent Lott. It was mailed to nearly 500,000 of his constituents; his office had worked with the National Center for Missing and Exploited Children to get some exposure for her case. They were hopeful that this would bring in some new leads, but unfortunately, no new information was learned.

By 1992, Daffany's case had gone cold. It remained inactive for years; detectives weren't assigned to re-investigate it until 1998. All of those who had worked on the case admitted it was a heartbreaking one, and they fervently wished they could solve it and give Daffany's family some closure.

Although Daffany had been missing for a decade at that point, Shirley still hoped that there was a chance she might be found alive somewhere. Her attitude towards Ernest had softened over the years; she no longer believed that he had anything to do with her granddaughter's disappearance. Although the timing seemed to point to Ernest, he had voluntarily submitted to a polygraph about the case and had passed.

Robbie, who claimed she failed her initial polygraph because she was still so emotional about Daffany's disappearance, agreed to take a second polygraph when she was a little calmer, and she passed as well. With no evidence pointing toward Robbie or Ernest, detectives moved on to pursue other leads. Unfortunately, investigators were unable to develop any new suspects

145

and the case once again went cold.

Daffany's family seemed to come to terms with the fact that she was likely no longer alive, but they still clung to a strand of hope that she might be found. For years, no new information came in concerning Daffany's disappearance, but the family continued to pray that the case would be solved. In 2007, they thought their prayers were answered: a woman was located that some believed was Daffany.

The woman in question spelled her first name as "Dafany" but was the same age Daffany would be and looked like several of the Tullos family members. A search of vital records failed to find any record of her mother giving birth to her, leading some to speculate she was indeed the missing girl. Detectives quickly determined it wasn't Daffany, however, and the family's hopes were once again shattered.

On the 30th anniversary of Daffany's disappearance, Shirley – 81 years old at the time – told reporters that she just wanted to know what happened to her granddaughter. She notes that it is all the unknowns about the case that hurt the most, and she hopes to find some closure before she dies.

Daffany's disappearance received a lot of attention from the local news media right from the beginning due to an odd coincidence: she went missing on the same day that Annie Laurie Hearin, a 71-year-old Jackson woman who was married to one of Mississippi's wealthiest men, was kidnapped from her home. A ransom note was left behind, and though Ralph Hearin paid the $1 million the kidnappers demanded, his wife was never seen again. Both Daffany and Annie were often featured together since they vanished from the same city just hours apart; although both cases remain unsolved, detectives have never believed that they were at all related.

Daffany Tullos was just 7 years old when she went missing from Jackson, Mississippi in July 1988. She has brown eyes and black hair, and at the time of her disappearance, she was 3 feet 7 inches tall and weighed 55 pounds. She was last seen wearing white shorts and a sleeveless blue shirt; she was not wearing shoes. All of her clothing had her name written on the tag. Daffany suffered from epileptic seizures and was on medication for it, but did not have her medication with her when she vanished. If you have any information about Daffany, please contact the Jackson Police Department at 601-960-1234 or the FBI at 202-324-3000.

Darlene Webb

Darlene Webb agreed to go to a nightclub with some friends on Friday, January 21, 1983, but told them that she couldn't stay out too late. The 20-year-old had recently been promoted to an assistant manager position at Chick-fil-A, in Daytona Beach, Florida, and she needed to be at work early on Saturday morning. The manager of the store was sick with the flu; Darlene had dropped off some chicken soup at his house on Friday afternoon and he asked if she could open the restaurant for him the following morning. She had been more than happy to take on the extra shift and promised her manager that she would make sure the store opened on time.

In addition to working at Chick-fil-A, Darlene was a student at Daytona Beach Community College. The college was located just 10 miles away from the home Darlene shared with her mother and brother, and Darlene had recently bought a 1981 Chevrolet Chevette so she could drive herself to school and work.

On Friday night, Darlene made the six-mile drive from her home to the Beachcomber Club, a popular gathering place in Daytona Beach. She parked her white Chevette near the corner of North Grandview Avenue and Seabreeze Boulevard; from there she walked a few blocks until she reached the nightclub, located on North Atlantic Avenue. She met her friends there, and they spent the rest of the evening talking and dancing.

It was 1:30 am by the time the group finally left the club, and Darlene knew she was going to be tired in the morning. Although the friends started walking to their cars together, Darlene was parked the furthest from the Beachcomber, so she walked the final block to her car alone. She made it safely back to her Chevette and tossed her purse onto the passenger seat. She should have been home by 1:45 am, but she never got there.

Darlene's mother, Fran Webb, wasn't initially concerned when Darlene didn't return home that night. She would occasionally stay with a friend if she stayed out too late, and Fran assumed that was what she had done. She went to bed believing that Darlene would likely be home by the time she woke up the following morning.

Early Saturday morning, Fran was startled awake by the sound of the phone ringing. It was Darlene's manager from Chick-fil-A, and he wanted to know why Darlene had not shown up to open the restaurant. In an instant, Fran knew that something was horribly wrong. Her daughter was known for being extremely dependable, and she had never missed a shift at work. She immediately hung up with Darlene's manager and started calling the friends her daughter had been out with the previous night.

None of Darlene's friends had seen her since they parted ways outside the club, but they knew the approximate area where she had parked her car. Several of her friends volunteered to drive to Daytona Beach to look for the Chevette; they found it in the same place where Darlene had indicated she was parked. Her purse could be seen inside the car, but there was no sign of Darlene.

The Chevette's front passenger side window was rolled halfway down, and the seat was reclined as if someone had been sitting in it. Most disturbing to Darlene's friends was the fact that the car's ashtray was filled with cigarette butts. Darlene was not a smoker, nor were any of her friends. They didn't believe she would willingly let anyone smoke in her car.

Fearing the worst, Fran called the Daytona Beach Police Department to report her daughter missing. Police were unable to find any signs of foul play in or around Darlene's car, and they initially assumed that she most likely left voluntarily. As they learned more about Darlene, however, they re-evaluated their original assumption and indicated to the news media that her disappearance was suspicious.

Three days after Darlene was reported missing, police issued a statewide bulletin so that law enforcement in all other Florida jurisdictions would be aware that she was missing. They also appealed to the public for help in locating Darlene. Although they still had no evidence to indicate foul play had occurred, they noted that she was not the kind of person who would voluntarily disappear without having any sort of contact with her family. She had not taken any of her belongings with her; the only items missing from her car had been her car keys. Everything else was located, including her wallet, indicating that robbery was not a likely motive. If foul play was involved, it appeared Darlene herself was the target.

Detectives interviewed Darlene's family members, friends, and classmates. None of them believed that Darlene would have chosen to disappear on her own, and no one could think of anyone who had any reason to want to harm the missing woman. She didn't live a high-risk lifestyle, spending most of her time at school, work, or with family. Although her parents were separated, she maintained a good relationship with both of them.

Darlene's family described her as someone who was always happy and positive, though she could be tough when she needed to be. She had a beautiful voice, but would sometimes start singing songs in an off-key voice just to make her friends and family members smile. She had been pleased about earning a promotion at work and was looking forward to completing college.

To make sure the public knew that Darlene was missing, her family made up missing posters with her picture and placed them in all the area businesses. They didn't see how it was possible for Darlene to disappear without someone seeing something, and they prayed for anyone who might have witnessed something to come forward and tell police what they knew. If anyone had any knowledge about Darlene, they remained silent.

A woman who had been working at a beer garden near where Darlene parked her car told police that she heard a woman's scream the night that Darlene went missing. She stopped what she was doing and looked in the direction she believed the scream had come from, but didn't hear anything else. She did observe a car speeding away from the area with its lights off, but she had been unable to determine what type of car it was or how many people were inside. Police thanked her for coming forward, but were unable to determine if the scream or the speeding car had anything to do with the missing woman.

Investigators continued to appeal to the public for information, but Darlene had seemingly vanished into thin air. There were a few people who called in claiming they saw the missing woman, but none of the sightings could be verified. Her family insisted that Darlene would never voluntarily go this long without contacting her family; they believed she had been taken against her will. They were unwilling to accept the fact that she might be dead, however, believing instead that she was alive but suffering from some sort of memory loss that rendered her incapable of remembering her own name. It seemed an unlikely theory to police; as more time went by, they believed that Darlene had most likely been murdered.

In 1984, a streetcleaner came forward and told police that he had seen two men forcing a woman into a car in Daytona Beach on the night Darlene disappeared. This was in line with the theory that Darlene had been abducted, but the streetcleaner had no explanation for why he had waited so long to come forward. He was unable to provide descriptions of the men, woman, or the car involved, so police were never sure if there was any connection between his claim and Darlene's disappearance.

Two years after Darlene went missing, police still had no idea what had happened to her. They had not received many tips and were unable to develop any real leads. They believed foul play was likely, but had no suspects or persons of interest.

Fran had still not given up hope of finding her daughter alive. Her porch light had been left on since Darlene went missing; the last person who came home at night was supposed to turn it off, and since Darlene never came home, it was still burning. Fran admitted that she went through more lightbulbs than she used to, but was adamant that the light would remain on until her daughter was located.

Darlene's family continued to hang up Darlene's missing posters and offered a reward for information that led to her recovery. Her younger brother, Jim, spent most nights roaming the streets of Daytona Beach, hoping to find any sort of clue that would lead to his sister.

Fran made sure there were gifts for Darlene under the Christmas tree each year, and she continued to sign Darlene's name on cards and gifts given by the family. She saw it as a way to keep her part of their everyday life.

Frustrated by the lackadaisical way most police departments appeared to investigate reports of missing adults, Fran decided to form a support group for parents whose adult children had gone missing. Fran felt that society usually ignored missing adult cases, assuming that the victim had done something that made them responsible for their own disappearances. There were numerous groups in existence to help find missing children, but few that aided families of missing adults. She hoped that the group, Mothers Aid to Missing Adults, would draw attention to the problem of missing adults in America as well as support families that were dealing with a missing loved one.

Although Darlene's family was desperate to find her, it was clear by 1985 that the investigation into her disappearance had gone cold. Police still had no persons of interest or suspects; they didn't believe that Darlene left voluntarily, but could find no one with any motive to want to harm her. It appeared that she had been the victim of a random act of violence. Unfortunately, stranger abductions are notoriously hard to solve, and detectives admitted that unless someone with first-hand knowledge of the case stepped forward, the chances of finding Darlene were slim.

The case remained cold and inactive for over 20 years before investigators learned of a possible lead. In July 2006, the Los Angeles Police Department released more than 80 photographs that had been seized from the home of William Richard Bradford in 1984. Bradford was arrested and later convicted of killing a teenage neighbor, but authorities had long suspected he might be a serial killer. He had traveled throughout the country claiming he could help women get a start in the modeling industry, and he took numerous photographs of potential models during his cross-country travels. Police released the photographs in an attempt to identify the women to see if any of them might have been unknown victims of Bradford.

One of the photographs showed a woman who looked a lot like Darlene, and Fran believed there was a possibility it was her daughter. Police were aware that Bradford had traveled through Daytona Beach on more than one occasion, and theorized that Darlene might have become one of his victims.

Unfortunately, Bradford died in San Quentin prison in 2006. While some of the women he photographed have since been found alive, one of those photographed was eventually identified as Donnalee Duhamel. Her decapitated corpse had been discovered in Malibu in 1978; at the time authorities had not been able to determine her identity and she was buried as a Jane Doe. She had met Bradford in a bar a few days before her corpse was found.

Most of the women photographed by Bradford remain unidentified, and it's still unknown if Darlene was one of his victims. While her family believed Darlene was shown in one of his photographs, police determined that the picture was taken in California after studying some of the things that appeared in the background. Although it's possible Bradford abducted Darlene in Florida and took her to California, police do not think this is a likely scenario.

There has been no progress made on Darlene's case in recent years, and what happened to her that night remains a complete mystery. She is almost certainly dead, but her family has continued to search for her and will not stop until they can bring her home.

Darlene Webb was just 20 years old when she went missing from Daytona Beach, Florida in January 1983. She has brown eyes and brown hair, and at the time of her disappearance, she was 5 feet 6 inches tall and weighed approximately 125 pounds. She was last seen wearing a white blouse, a printed skirt, and flat shoes. She was wearing three necklaces; a gold and diamond one engraved with her name, one with a Virgin Mary pendant, and a gold one with a buttercup pendant that had a small diamond embedded in it. Her ears are pierced and she has a burn scar on her left hand. If you have any information about Darlene, please contact the Daytona Beach Police Department at 386-671-5100.

Brandi Wells

Brandi Wells was looking forward to a night out before she had to start classes for the fall semester. Graham Central Station, a nightclub in Longview, Texas, offered Ladies' Night specials on Wednesday nights; she decided to go there on the evening of August 2, 2006. She left her Brownsboro, Texas apartment and made the 30-minute drive to her mother's house in Tyler, Texas. She was hoping that her younger sister would go to the club with her, but she wasn't feeling well and was already in bed when Brandi arrived. Not wanting to miss out on her final chance to have some fun before she returned to school, Brandi made the decision to go to the club alone. She never returned home.

At 23 years old, Brandi was finally getting her life back on track. She was a graduate of Chapel Hill High School, where she had been a member of the band and the flag corps; she was talented enough that she received a college scholarship to the University of Texas at Tyler. Although she had done well in her freshman year, she fell in love and decided to get married at the age of 19. She continued going to college but soon found that she couldn't balance her school and her home life, so she dropped out after completing her sophomore year. She promised herself that she would go back to school one day to realize her dream of becoming a teacher, but after her marriage ended in divorce she moved to San Antonio to regroup and put her dream of going back to college on hold.

Brandi had recently returned to East Texas and decided to enroll at Trinity Valley Community College. She was a little nervous about going back to college because she was a few years older than most of her classmates, but she was excited at the same time. She was going to be participating in band front again, and she was looking forward to the start of band camp the following week.

Brandi had been having some financial difficulties, but she had just been hired at a local Walmart and was pleased that she would have a steady paycheck. Prior to finding employment, she had been considering going to a pawn shop to see how much money she could get for some of her items of jewelry. Everything in her life seemed to be coming together nicely, and she was looking forward to what the future would bring.

Brandi's mother, Ellen Tant, was pleasantly surprised when Brandi showed up at her home that Wednesday night. She hoped her daughter would stay and visit for a while, but Brandi was determined to go out that night, with or without her sister. She got changed into a dark, floral-printed tube top and rust-colored gaucho pants, then carefully applied her make-up. She completed her outfit with a pair of high-heeled sandals, then emerged from the bathroom and asked her mother how she looked. Ellen told her she looked adorable.

Before she left, Brandi asked her mother if she could borrow her car for the night, as her own car was low on gas. Ellen didn't have much gas in her car either so she refused to lend it to her. Brandi left the house in her own 2000 Pontiac Grand Prix; her mother assumed that she was going to one of the local nightclubs in Tyler.

Before heading to the club, Brandi stopped at a nearby bowling alley where a family friend, Jenette Green, worked as a bartender. Brandi told Jenette that her mother said she could order a drink and charge it to Ellen's tab, and Jenette made her a cherry vodka sour. As she sat at the bar with her drink, Brandi told Jenette about her plans for the night. She was heading to Graham Central Station, located about 45 minutes away. She had never been there before but wanted to check it out because it sounded like a fun place.

Jenette warned Brandi to be careful, especially as she wasn't familiar with the Longview area and didn't really seem to know where she was going. Brandi shrugged her off with a smile and told her she would be fine. She only finished about half her drink before she told Jenette she was leaving and would see her later. With a final wave, she walked out of the door.

Despite Brandi's assurances that she would be fine, she didn't really know where she was going and made several phone calls to Graham Central Station during her drive; she apparently made at least one wrong turn and needed to confirm directions to the nightclub. She eventually found her way there and entered the club around 10:30 pm.

Although Brandi had told her mother that she was going to be meeting some friends at the club, this does not appear to be the case. Brandi did ask a couple of people – her sister and her godmother – if they wanted to go to Graham Central Station with her, but most of her friends had no idea about her plans. Ellen believed Brandi was meeting up with some of her old high school friends at a club in Tyler, but none of them had spoken to Brandi about going out that night.

Brandi was recorded on surveillance video entering Graham Central Station alone, and she was seen leaving alone around 12:30 am. She spoke with several people inside the club, but she didn't run into anyone she knew.

It's unclear if she had anything to drink while she was there, but those who spoke to her recalled that she appeared sober. She did seem to be extremely concerned about the fact that she was almost out of gas, and while she didn't directly ask anyone for money, one man said she hinted that she could use some money for gas.

When Ellen woke up on Thursday morning, Brandi wasn't at the house. Ellen wasn't particularly concerned and assumed that Brandi had too much to drink the night before and stayed with a friend. Since she no longer lived in her mother's home, she likely wouldn't have felt it necessary to update Ellen on her overnight plans.

Brandi lived with a roommate in Brownsboro, and her roommate grew concerned when Brandi hadn't returned by Thursday evening and called Ellen to see if she was still there. It was at that point that Ellen started to worry, and she began calling her daughter's cell phone. She left several frantic voicemail messages without getting a reply.

There was still no word from Brandi by Friday morning, and Ellen started to panic. Although Brandi was an adult, it was unlike her to be out of contact for so long; she was normally very responsive to voicemail and text messages. Ellen continued trying to call her, but by that afternoon Brandi's voicemail was full and she could no longer leave messages. Ellen then called the police to report her missing.

An officer from the Tyler Police Department came to the house to take a missing person report. Ellen was still under the impression that Brandi had gone to the Electric Cowboy, a nightclub located just blocks away from their home, and that was what she told police. Brandi's sister corrected her, telling her mother that Brandi had planned to drive to Longview and go to Graham Central Station.

Ellen and Brandi's godmother, Michelle Cole, worried that Brandi might have run into car trouble on her drive to or from Longview, especially as she had mentioned she was low on gas. Ellen was annoyed that Brandi hadn't told her she planned to drive so far away; she likely knew her mother wouldn't have approved of the idea.

Once Tyler Police learned that Brandi had likely gone missing from Longview, they told Ellen that she needed to call the police there. Ellen did so, but the Longview Police Department didn't seem at all concerned and told Ellen that her daughter was an adult who could come and go as she pleased; they weren't going to search for someone who had most likely taken off voluntarily.

Brandi's family and friends were convinced that she hadn't run away, and they launched their own search for her. While Ellen stayed at the house and started calling all of Brandi's friends, Michelle decided to make the 45-minute drive to Graham Central Station. She searched the parking lot and surrounding area for any sign of Brandi or her car but found nothing.

Sadly, when Michelle went to Longview to look for Brandi's car, it had already been located but hadn't been connected to the missing person case. A trooper from the Texas Department of Public Safety spotted the car parked on the side of Interstate 20 just outside of Longview on Thursday morning, its driver's side door partially open. He pulled in behind the car around 9:00 am and ran the license plate number; once he determined it hadn't been stolen and wasn't wanted in connection with any crime, he assumed it had simply broken down on the highway. He tagged it as abandoned; if the owner didn't return for it, it would eventually be towed.

Brandi hadn't been reported missing yet at the

time the car was found; once the missing person report was filed, it would still take days before law enforcement realized the connection between Brandi and the abandoned Grand Prix. By this point, the car had been sitting on the side of the road for five days.

Investigators searched the car and the area surrounding it on August 8th. They found nothing inside the car or in the immediate area that indicated a struggle had taken place. Brandi's purse and wallet were found in the backseat, along with a cell phone and a napkin with a man's name and phone number on it. The driver's seat had been pushed all the way back as if to accommodate a very tall driver; Brandi herself was only 4 feet 11 inches and would have been unable to drive the car with the seat in that position.

In the trunk of the car, detectives discovered a gas can that Ellen didn't believe belonged to her daughter; this seemed to suggest that Brandi did indeed run out of gas and might have asked for help from someone she thought was a good Samaritan.

Since they now believed that Brandi might have been a victim of foul play, detectives finally launched an investigation into her disappearance. They called the man whose phone number Brandi had written down on a napkin, and he confirmed that he had seen her at Graham Central Station on Wednesday night and talked to her for a while. He had offered to buy her a drink, but she declined; she mentioned that she was concerned about running out of gas and left the club shortly after that. He had not spoken to her again.

Detectives were sent to Graham Central Station, and they learned that the club would swipe the identification card of every patron as they entered, and they were able to determine the exact time that Brandi's

161

license had been swiped. The club was equipped with several surveillance cameras, and they provided police with the footage from the night Brandi disappeared.

Detectives viewed the footage from around the time Brandi's license had been swiped and saw a woman who appeared to be Brandi talking with two men who arrived with her. Unsure if the woman on video was the missing woman, they asked for a family member to come down to the police station to view the surveillance footage. Ellen was too upset to go but sent several other family members instead. They agreed with police that the woman was indeed Brandi.

Police released the relevant surveillance footage to the news media, hoping to learn the identity of the two men seen with Brandi. Although they received numerous tips, none of them led to Brandi or either of the men. When Ellen saw the video, however, she wasn't convinced that the woman in question was actually her daughter. Although the woman looked similar to her daughter and had the same build, the clothing the woman was wearing was not what Brandi had left the house in that night.

A few weeks later, Ellen's sister and brother-in-law went to the Longview Police station to watch the video, and within minutes they spotted Brandi – but it wasn't the woman previously identified as their niece. It turned out that the time stamp on the surveillance video was nine minutes off from that of the ID swiping machine.

When Ellen saw the new footage, she was certain that it showed Brandi. She was wearing the clothing that she remembered Brandi changing into, and she arrived and left Graham Central Station alone. As she exited the club, however, an unidentified man wearing a white cowboy hat could be seen leaving right behind her. He appeared to head off in a different direction than Brandi did as he entered the parking lot, but he did glance toward her; immediately after Brandi moved out of the view of the surveillance camera, a shadow can be seen that seems to indicate she changed direction and headed towards this unknown male. Attempts at identifying this man were unsuccessful and it is unknown if he was at all connected with Brandi's disappearance. There were no cameras in the parking lot.

Detectives called all the contacts listed in the cell phone they found in the back of Brandi's car, which they assumed belonged to the missing woman. Some of the people they called knew who Brandi was, but others didn't. They were confused about this; it wasn't until they finally showed Ellen the cell phone that she was able to clear up the mystery for them: it wasn't Brandi's phone. It had belonged to her ex-boyfriend who was now in the military. Detectives had spent more than a week trying to track down leads from the wrong cell phone. Brandi's cell phone was not found in her car, leading them to wonder if she might have taken off voluntarily after all.

Once they obtained cell phone records for Brandi's phone, they discovered something disturbing. There was no activity on the phone at all for more than a week following her disappearance, but then a number of calls were made to and from her phone. Hundreds of calls, one right after the other, one to two minutes in length, suggested the phone might have been used by someone dealing drugs.

Authorities traced the phone to a man and his niece, who said they had been given the phone by a third man; this man claimed that he had found the phone on the ground on August 11th and simply decided to start using it. This man, whose name has never been released, had a criminal record and police were already familiar with him. The location where he claimed he found the phone was in a very high crime area about four blocks away from the highway where Brandi's car was found; it is unlikely the phone would have gone unnoticed on the ground there for nine days before being found.

The man and his niece agreed to submit to polygraph examinations regarding Brandi's disappearance, and they passed. The man who claimed he found the phone, however, initially refused to be polygraphed; later reports indicate that he finally agreed to take one but he failed. He is a person of interest in the case, but police do not have any evidence directly linking him to Brandi's disappearance.

Over the years, there have been a number of searches conducted for Brandi, but there have never been any clues found that point to what might have happened to her. There are a number of theories, but no evidence to support or disprove any of them. Members of her family fear that she was abducted and forced into the sex trade industry; they do not want to think about the possibility that she was killed and still hope that she might be found alive. Ellen refuses to stop searching for her daughter and will not give up until she knows what happened to her.

Brandi Wells was just 23 years old when she went missing from Longview, Texas in August 2006. She has brown eyes and brown hair, and at the time of her disappearance, she was 4 feet 11 inches tall and weighed 120 pounds. She was last seen wearing a dark-colored tube top with a floral print, rust-colored gaucho pants, and black high-heeled sandals. If you have any information about Brandi, please contact the Longview Police Department at 903-237-1110.

Alan & Terry Westerfield

Residents of Fayetteville, North Carolina woke up to a beautiful, sunny morning on Saturday, September 12, 1964, but anyone who had listened to the weather forecast knew that it wasn't going to last. Hurricane Dora had made landfall in Florida two days earlier and was currently raging through Georgia. Although North Carolina wasn't going to be hit nearly as hard as the states to the south, heavy rainfall and winds were projected to move into the area late that night.

Terry and Alan Westerfield lived on Madison Avenue in Fayetteville, and they were home alone that Saturday because their mother, Margie, was at work in a local beauty parlor. It was an era when it was still somewhat rare for mothers to work outside the home, but Margie needed the income. She had been divorced from the boys' father, an army sergeant at Fort Jackson, South Carolina, since 1961. She had gotten remarried to a man named Carl Bock, but they had recently separated and he had moved out of the house.

Alan and Terry watched television for a while that morning before deciding to play outside for a while. Despite the age difference between them, the boys were extremely close, and 11-year-old Terry was fiercely protective of his seven-year-old brother. They enjoyed riding their bicycles around the neighborhood, and would sometimes join in with other children in the neighborhood playing Cowboys and Indians alongside the railroad tracks.

If Terry and Alan thought they would have an

entire day free of adult supervision, they were wrong. Around 11:00 am, Carl Bock came to the house. It's unclear why their soon-to-be ex-stepfather decided to spend the day at the house; Margie was unaware he was planning on being there. Both Terry and Alan went home at some point, most likely to eat lunch. Some of the neighborhood children knocked on their door that afternoon and asked Carl if Alan could come back outside and play some more. Carl told them that Alan was in his room being punished for something and was not allowed outside. Neighbors recall seeing Terry outside riding his bike until around 1:00 pm, but then he went back inside as well.

Around 4:40 pm, a neighbor saw Carl driving away from the house. He returned a short time later and said that he had dropped the boys off at the Broadway Theater in town so they could watch a double feature. He dropped them off at the front of the theater and told them he would be back to pick them up around 8:00 pm. When Margie got home from work at 5:30 pm, Carl was there and he told her that the boys were at the movies for the night. If he was hoping that the alone time would help him and Margie rekindle their romance, he was quite mistaken. Margie rarely had any kid-free nights, so she decided to take advantage of it and made plans to go out for the evening with one of her girlfriends.

Around 7:45 pm, Carl left the house and drove to the theater to pick up Alan and Terry. He pulled his car into a no-parking zone where he had a good view of the doors to the theater and waited. He claims that he sat there until 9:30 pm, but there was no sign of the boys. Deciding that Margie must have picked them up, he went back to the house on Madison Avenue and waited. Margie returned to the house around 1:00 am and found Carl there, but not Alan and Terry. When he told her that he hadn't been able to find the boys, she was frantic with worry and immediately called the police. By this time, the expected rain had moved in, flooding certain areas of the town and knocking out power and some of the telephone lines in town as well. Fayetteville police came to the house to get Margie and drove to the theater with her. The manager met them there and unlocked the doors for them. They were hoping that perhaps the boys had somehow fallen asleep during the movie and had been inadvertently locked inside. After a thorough search of the theater, though, they were positive that the boys were not inside.

Morning came without any sign of the missing boys. Investigators wondered if the boys' father had somehow been involved, perhaps picking them up and taking them home with him. Margie tried to convince herself that the police were right, that somehow Tom Westerfield had decided to pick up his sons for an impromptu visit. It was an unlikely scenario – even if he had come to Fayetteville for the boys, there was no way he could have known about their movie outing – but it would mean that the boys were alive and unharmed. Detectives reached Tom at the army base in South Carolina, but he told them he didn't have the boys and had no idea what could have happened to them. The sheriff was able to verify Tom's alibi; he hadn't been anywhere near North Carolina the previous night. Margie had known it was a long shot, but the news that Tom didn't have the boys was too much for her to take. She went into shock and completely broke down. She would end up spending the next two weeks in the psychiatric ward of Womack Army Hospital.

While Margie was in the hospital struggling to

comprehend what could have happened to her boys, detectives turned their attention to Carl Bock. He had been the last person to see the boys, and that would have been enough to arouse police suspicions even if he weren't in the process of separating from the boys' mother. He was subject to intense scrutiny, and was questioned by detectives on multiple occasions. His story never wavered. He insisted that he had dropped the boys off at the movies somewhere around 4:40 pm.

Due to the young ages of the boys and the fact that there had been a possible abduction, the FBI entered the case almost immediately. Police made a public appeal for anyone who had any information regarding the boys to please come forward, but it appeared that no one had seen anything odd the day that the boys had disappeared. Detectives were unable to come up with any leads in the case. The fact that the area was still being hammered with torrential downpours didn't help any. Flooding in the area would have washed away any potential evidence, making it impossible for investigators to find footprints or any other evidence leading to the location of the boys.

Unfortunately, Alan and Terry's case quickly went cold. Police were never able to uncover any new leads, and the bodies of the boys have never been found. Many people, both detectives and family members, believed that Carl Bock was responsible for the boys' disappearance. They felt that the boys were dead long before Carl claimed to have dropped them off at the theater. But with no physical evidence linking him to the crime – and with him sticking to the same story and denying involvement – they were unable to charge him with anything.

The Westerfield case has been unsolved for more than 50 years now. But was it really an unsolvable case? Obviously, advances in technology have made case investigations much more sophisticated than they used to be, and we can't fault the investigators for the relatively primitive tools they had to work with. But a look at the investigation raises more questions than answers. Carl Bock was alone in the house with Alan and Terry for a few hours on that fateful Saturday. It's clear that some people believe that the boys never made it out of their house alive that day, and that Carl likely killed them and then made up the story about taking the boys to the movies. It's unclear, however, if investigators did a thorough search of the house or Carl's car. The driving rains of Hurricane Dora may have been enough to wash away any signs of footprints, and flooding could have made it difficult to locate any places where a freshly dug grave could have been, but any evidence inside the house or car wouldn't have been affected by the rain.

The Broadway Theater didn't have any kind of surveillance camera that could prove if the boys actually made it to the theater that day, making it impossible to verify Carl's story. But Alan and Terry loved going to the movies and were frequent patrons of the theater – frequent patrons who were known to the majority of the employees that worked there. Not a single employee reported seeing the boys at the theater that night. Terry, with his bright red hair, would have been especially hard to miss. If the boys were never in the theater that day, it would cast doubt on everything that Carl claimed had taken place.

Some of the boys' family members believed that the police were covering for Carl because he had law enforcement experience. As an army sergeant, Carl was involved with the military police and he worked for the criminal investigation division at Fort Bragg. There is no evidence that backs up the claim that there was a police cover-up, but it's possible that Carl didn't need one. If he worked on criminal investigations, it can be assumed that he knew a lot about crime scenes – and how to cover his tracks.

It's clear that Carl had both the motive and the opportunity necessary to commit the crime. He and Margie were no longer together, and if he wanted to hurt her, the best way of doing so was through her children. He was alone in the house with them all afternoon, which would have given him plenty of time to commit the crime.

But if Carl did murder Alan and Terry, where did he hide the bodies? It doesn't appear that he left the immediate area for very long that day, which would limit the distance he could have traveled to dispose of the bodies. There was an intense manhunt in the days following the disappearances, but investigators found absolutely no trace of the boys or evidence of a crime, and the fact that the bodies were never found ensured that the case never went to trial. This can lead to a couple of different conclusions. It's possible the bodies have never been found because Carl managed to somehow discover the perfect hiding spot. Or it could be that there were never any bodies to find in the first place. Although it seems highly unlikely, there is always a chance that the boys did leave on their own. We have no way of knowing what took place in the boys' home that day, but perhaps Carl did something that led them to believe that running away would be the only way they could escape from him.

Alan and Terry Westerfield remain listed as missing persons, and their case is open and unsolved. While detectives may never be able to determine just what happened to the boys, they would still like to be able to locate their bodies to give their family some small measure of closure.

Alan John Westerfield was just 7 years old when he vanished from Fayetteville, North Carolina in September 1964. He has blue eyes and brown hair, and at the time of his disappearance, he was 3 feet 10 inches tall and weighed 80 pounds. Terry Lee Westerfield was just 11 years old when he vanished with his younger brother. He has blue eyes and red hair, and at the time of his disappearance, he was 4 feet 7 inches tall and weighed 90 pounds. If you have any information about Alan and Terry, please contact the Cumberland County Sheriff's Office at 910-323-1500.

Printed in Great Britain
by Amazon

35345641R00096